TASTING BRAZIL

ALSO BY JESSICA B. HARRIS

Hot Stuff: A Cookbook in Praise of the Piquant
Iron Pots & Wooden Spoons: Africa's Gifts to New World Cooking
Sky Juice and Flying Fish : Traditional Caribbean Cooking

TASTING
BRAZIL

Regional Recipes

and Reminiscences

JESSICA B. HARRIS

Macmillan Publishing Company • New York
Maxwell Macmillan Canada • Toronto

Maxwell Macmillan International
New York   Oxford   Singapore   Sydney

Macmillan Publishing Company
866 Third Avenue
New York, NY 10022

Maxwell Macmillan Canada, Inc.
1200 Eglinton Avenue East
Suite 200
Don Mills, Ontario M3C 3N1

Macmillan Publishing Company is part of
the Maxwell Communication Group of Companies.

Library of Congress Cataloging-in-Publication Data
Harris, Jessica B.
    Tasting Brazil: regional recipes and reminiscences/Jessica B.
Harris.
        p.   cm.
    Includes index.
ISBN 0-02-548261-0
    1. Cookery, Brazilian. I. Title.
    TX716.B6H37 1992   91-45729   CIP
    641.5981—dc20

Macmillan books are available at special discounts
for bulk purchase for sales promotions,
fund-raising, or educational use. For details, contact:

Special Sales Director
Macmillan Publishing Company
866 Third Avenue
New York, NY 10022

10 9 8 7 6 5 4 3 2 1

Printed in the United States of America

To my mother,

Rhoda A. Harris (Oxalá),

who stepped off the plane and knew intuitively why I fell in love with a country. Her mastery of the mysteries of the skillet and the saucepan and her "Boa Mão" gave me the desire to cook and her ever-adventurous spirit the desire to know why.

And to the memory of my father,

Jesse B. Harris–*ibae* (Xangô),

who lives on in the worldly conversation of Rio's drawing rooms, the roar of Iguaçu Falls, and the sound of drums in Bahian *terreiros*.

And to my Brazilian brothers,

Antonio Luiz Figuereido (Oxóssi),

whose quicksilver feet have led me to the foods, *feiras*, folk, and friends of Bahia and most importantly to their *orixás*.

And Marcelo Figuereido (Logunedé),

who is quite simply always there at the right moment.

—AXÉ

Acknowledgments

If no man is an island, then surely no cookbook writer can pick up a pen without first acknowledging those who went before. I could not have begun to research *Tasting Brazil* without the works of numerous Brazilian culinary historians, cookbook authors, and recorders of the history and development of the country. So to Alberto de Sampaio, Luis de Camara Cascudo, Antonio Houaiss, Gilberto Freye, Guilherme Figuereido, Pierre Verger, Darwin Brandão, Hildegardes Vianna, Raul Lody, Manuel Querino, Dona Benta, and the hundreds of nameless native Brazilian women, *mães pretas*, *iya basses*, cooks, and housekeepers over the centuries—*Muito, muito obrigada*.

Then, there are the more personal debts of gratitude, those that grow from meals shared, memories made, and time spent.

In Bahia

Axé and *Adupé* to all of the *filhas do santo*, *ogãs*, and *alabes* at Ile Iyá Nasso—Casa Branca do Engenho Velho—especially Mãe Tata, Mãe Tetê, Mãe Zurica, Mãe Vovô, Mãe Caetana, Mãe Nitinha, Kutu de Ogun, Maria de Ogun, Nair de Oxossi, *iyá basse* Naim, Sinha, Jorge, Valnisia, Te, and Peligro.

Axé and *Adupé* to all who celebrate *orixá* in the colonial city on the Bay including Mãe Menininha–*ibae*, Mãe Cleuza, and Mãe Regina at

Gantois, Mãe Stela at Axé Apô Afonjá, and Pierre Verger, Carybé, Pai Balbinho, Pai Cordero, and others.

Abraços carinhosos to Yêdamaría, Daria, Carminha, Noella, Luiz Carlos, Regina Celi, Yeda, Aline, Clarindo Silva, Neto, Tereza, Bianca, Pablo, and others.

Muito obrigado and *Abraços muito carinhosos.*

In Rio

To my Carioca "family" Guilherme and Alba Figuereido, who opened the ways and smoothed paths.

To Antonio Olinto and Zora Seljian, new friends with old wisdom.

To Vera Dodebi and Itamara Koorax, my new Brazilian "sisters," with affection and gratitude for their sharing.

To Antonio Houaiss, for his encouragement.

And to Rebecca Schwartz and Flavio Ferreira, new and old friends.

In São Paulo

To Nair de Carvalho, the gentle artist who was one of the first to walk with me on this path, with special thanks for introductions to Jorge Amado, Carybé, and Pierre Verger.

To Inaicyra, dancer extraordinaire, in whose blood runs that of African queens.

In New York

To Marlene Schwartz who put me on a plane and sent me to a *terra maravilhosa* for the first time.

At Varig Brazilian Airlines to Jackie Ingram with thanks for friendship and advice, to Jerry Yano and to Bobbi Schlesinger and K.T. with thanks and thoughts of the old days and a smile to Carlos for telling me where to sit.

To Erminha Apolinario with many, many thanks for Portuguese lessons which enabled me to *falar com gente*, recipes shared, and advice given.

To the folk at Via Brasil for recreating a tiny bit of Brasil up north.

The food crew who comes to eat, comment, and eat again must also be thanked, so thanks go to Richard Alleman, Brenda and Diane Blackman, June, Robert and Kamau Bobb, Lurita Brown, Karen Clark, Linda Cohen, Lynne and Patrick Eck, Ayoluwa Fenner, Patricia, Ja'nié and Anthony Hopkins, Patricia Lawrence, Karen

Kopta, Yvette and Ifelami Burgess Polcyn, Sandra Taylor, Cheikh Oumar Thiam, and the unnamed, but not forgotten one.

To the telephone support network who call, cajole, and send photocopies—Cathy Royal, Cynthia Bunton, William Woys Weaver, and Nancy Harmon Jenkins

And to Derrick Wright and Ron Cottman, who got me to market and kept the rain off.

A special thanks goes to Mable McCarthy and daughters Trisha and Mary Kay on Martha's Vineyard who provided freezer space and friendship when Hurricane Bob almost sabotaged the end of the book.

A big *abraço* and thanks go to my agent, Carole Abel, and my editor, Pam Hoenig, and her assistant, Justin Schwartz, who stopped my samba-ing and got me to sit at the computer long enough to get it done.

Finally, thanks again to my culinary secret weapon, my mother, without whom nothing would be possible.

Contents

TASTING BRAZIL

BRAZIL:
A Culinary History

Brazil is a country without a memory," says a leading guidebook on the subject. At times, indeed, it seems as if the monolithic country that occupies almost half of South America is too resolutely faced toward the future to think about its past. However, no country is without history. Whether hidden in musty tomes in archives or read in the words of scholars, debated by academics or decried by revolutionaries, it is unavoidably there. It is found in small everyday rites that frame a people and form future generations. In Brazil history is everywhere for those who look. It is there on the sun-dappled beaches that greeted the Portuguese and in the dense green interior that must have terrified them. It is in the cobbled streets of Pelourinho which tell more of colonial slavery than the records burned by Ruy Barbosa ever could. It is in the scorched earth of the Sertão and in the soaring buildings of Brasília. It is also in every bite of the country's food.

It tantalizes in the spice mixture that goes into the fish stews of the northeast, speaking of the native Brazilian love of ginger and lemon juice. It boldly recalls West Africa in the *dendê*—palm oil—malagueta pepper, and coconut milk that are the holy trinity of Afro-Bahian cooking, and Portugal in the *lingüiça*—sausage—and kale, or *couve*, that are found in hearty soups. In the south, it is found in each sip of coffee and in the multi-egg-yolked confections that hark back to Luisitanian convents and the Moorish occupation of the Iberian country. It is in every piece of sushi served in the Liberdade district of São Paulo and in each beer quaffed in Blumenau, each measure of cassava meal and each turn of the wooden spoon. All one has to do is look.

BRAZIL SARAVA

Palm trees, lots of palm trees bending toward Africa, piercingly blue sky with an occasional hint of cloud, white sandy beaches endlessly framing the horizon, and deep turquoise sea. So it must have seemed to Portuguese seaman Pedro Álvares Cabral and the crew of his ships on the twenty-second of April, 1500. No one is sure whether Cabral deliberately set sail to the west or was hopelessly blown off course; his original destination, the Cape of Good Hope, lay thousands of miles in the opposite direction. The Treaty of Tordesillas signed in 1494 had divided up the New World and given all lands known and unknown east of an imaginary north-south line 370 leagues west of the Cape Verde Islands to the Portuguese. The land which was thought to be an island therefore was claimed for Portugal and named Vera Cruz. When it was discovered that the land was indeed a part of a larger land mass, the name was changed to Santa Cruz. By 1511 maps show the name of this new colony had again been changed to reflect its major export: brazilwood, a dye much prized in Europe. Now the colony was known as Terra do Brasil.

When Cabral and his band of adventurers landed on the shores of Brazil somewhere between Porto Seguro and Bahia, they were greeted by bands of native Brazilians who welcomed them. Descendants of these first Brazilians, although their numbers are scarce today, still survive. There are enclaves where, protected by government edict, they live almost as they had in the time of Cabral. From them, and from the reports of travelers, we know about them and their diets.

FIRST THE INDIANS

Roots, Fruits, and Fresh, Fresh Fish

The Tupi-Guarani woman was charged with the upkeep of the entire household. Many of her culinary creations are still a part of the Brazilian culinary repertoire today. Gabriel Soares da Souza, a sixteenth-century chronicler, tells us that cassava was a main staple of the local diet. Women prepared cassava meal by scraping the roots of the plant with shells or shredding them with stone graters until they were white. The cassava pulp was then put into a woven tube called a *tapitim* which expressed the water and left dry cassava pulp. The pulp was then heated in a clay pot kept solely for that purpose and during cooking was stirred with a piece of calabash — gourd — so that it was evenly toasted. The toasted meal formed the basis for many dishes like tapioca and the sweet cassava and coconut crackers called *beijús*. Alternate methods called for soaking the cassava and then preparing the meal by expressing the water. The cassava liquid itself was also used and became the basis for tucupi, a condiment of cassava water, garlic, chile, chicory, and seasonings that is still prized in the Amazon region today.

Native Brazilians were familiar with the process of fermentation and they also prepared a variety of porridges known as *mingau*. Tupi women used leaves of local bananas called *pacova* for wrapping dishes prepared from cassava, coconut, rice, and corn, although the true banana arrived later and the use of its leaves did not become widespread until the arrival of African slaves later in the century.

The Portuguese mixed with the native Brazilians to a greater extent than colonists did in other places in the Western Hemisphere. Soon they too were eating corn porridges called *acanjic*, the origin of today's *canjica*, a hominy and coconut porridge, and *pamuna*, a green corn and coconut dessert steamed in cornhusks, today called *pamonha*. They snacked on *pipoca*, or popcorn, and sampled *pacoka*, or *paçoca*, the pulverized fish and cassava meal dish that has also given its name to a pulverized peanut and sugar candy. This dish was particularly popular as it could be kept for a long time and was useful for travelers and hunters.

Fish played a major role in the diet, with the place of honor going to the *pirarucú*, a giant Amazon fish. Other varieties from the tributaries of the great river were also eaten, as were manatees which were and are called *peixe boi,* or ox fish. It was preserved by sun drying or roasted in its own fat and stored in large pottery jars. Turtle was a delicacy and a variety of dishes were prepared from the meat and the eggs.

Green vegetables did not play a large role in the diet of the native Brazilians. Women did occasionally gather leafy greens which they used in stews. Other vegetables used included sweet potatoes and a few types of beans. Hearts of palm were a particular favorite and were eaten both raw and cooked with great relish. Fruits abounded, but the Tupi-Guarani seemed to be fond of only papaya and guava and cashew. The cashew wine of the northeastern region is a reminder of this love.

Condiments played an important role in the diet of the native Brazilians. In the sixteenth century, a Jesuit missionary explained that their immoderate use of "ginger, chile, and lemons was such that it gave them frequent attacks of dysentery." Indeed, in the native Brazilian diet, lemon juice frequently took the place of salt and the salt-and-pepper mixture known as *juquitaia.* Chiles were much loved and the many varieties of chiles available in the Amazon region, which is home to a vast number from the habanero chile family, are perhaps at the basis of the national chile mania today.

Another of the lasting contributions of the native Brazilians to the cooking of today's Brazil has certainly been its cooking utensils. The mortar, the earthen water jug, and the wicker sieve, as well as calabash gourd spoons and dippers that are found in Brazilian kitchens large and small all hark back to the inventiveness of these first Brazilians.

EUROPEAN ARRIVALS

Lusitanian Feasts and Famines

In 1533, when the Portuguese arrived in Brazil to colonize the region, they were confronted by a country so vast that it must have terrified the arrivals from the strip of land on the eastern section of the Iberian peninsula. Portugal at the time of the colonization of Brazil was a nation that was far from stable. It was, in fact, just recovering from a lengthy period of Moorish occupation, one that would mark mother country and colony alike with a taste of North Africa. The Moors had brought to Portugal their own customs, ranging from their blue-and-white tiles, known as *azulejos* in Spanish, through their science and technology in building, to their food. The former would serve as a decorative motif for the colonial kitchens of many a Brazilian great house. The second would afford the colonizers the know-how to construct water-driven sugar mills which processed the sugarcane that was the wealth of the colony in the seventeenth century. The third transformed the diet of Portugal and eventually of Brazil.

Old Portuguese cookbooks, such as *Arte de Cozinha* which was published in 1692 by a royal cook, are filled with recipes for "Moorish lamb," "Moorish fish," and the like. The North African conquerors brought with them citrus fruits, and the oranges, tangerines, and lemons were eaten fresh and preserved into dried fruits and comfits. Perhaps the greatest and most lasting legacy of the Moors was the North African sweet tooth. Visitors to Portugal in the sixteenth century commented on the country's excessive use of sugar and egg yolks.

According to historian Gilberto Freye, the years after the Moors were fraught with alternate feasting and fasting, as the diet of the Portuguese upper classes wavered between the excesses required on religious festival days and when meals had to be provided to royal retainers, rent collectors, and religious persons to give a good show, and those far more frequent days when the daily meal was little more than bread and radishes. For the poor, the diet was not even relieved by the occasional day of feasting; bread and onions were the norm and not the exception. The more fortunate had recourse to cooked sardines, the cheapest fish available. In short, "Brazil was colonized by a nation of the undernourished."

The only strongholds where food was had in abundance seem to have been in the monasteries and the convents where the continued cultivation of kitchen gardens and raising of fowl and small herds of domestic cattle allowed for more balanced fare.

Upon their arrival in Brazil, the colonizers were so preoccupied with acquiring fortunes that their diets did not improve markedly in the new, rich land. All was sacrificed to King Sugar, a hard taskmaster in its need for vast amounts of land. Cattle were banished, as they destroyed the sugarcane, and domestic agriculture was neglected in favor of the sugar-bearing grass.

The women brought with them the North African/Luisitanian art of preparing preserved fruits and confections and immediately set to work re-creating their favorite sweets using New World ingredients, as well as the traditional eggs and the sugar that made their husbands' fortunes. The inventively named sweets from Portuguese convents remained and nuns' sighs, maiden's drool, and heavenly bacon became part of the Brazilian menu.

However, the mythic figure of the plantation owner sitting down to a board groaning with fresh meat, home-cultivated vegetables, and fresh fruit is erroneous. In fact, most sat down to meals of stringy beef and fruits and vegetables aswarm with parasites and insects. The extremely wealthy were all too frequently the most foolish: they imported their food—meat, cereals, and even fruits—from Portugal and from the Azores. By the time it arrived, badly preserved and maggot-infested, it was nutritionally worth no more than the poor fare they already had.

With increased importance given to the cultivation of sugar, the diet grew even poorer and by the seventeenth century, travelers were astonished to notice that the large cities of the colony had no slaughterhouses because there were no cattle to send there. This was particularly true in the northeastern region where sugar reigned supreme. In the nonsugar-growing south, food was more abundant and of better quality. Freye even raises the question as to whether this may account for the prosperity of that region today.

The Portuguese in the northeastern region of the country learned much from the native Brazilians. They adopted the use of cassava meal almost immediately in preference to the wheat flour of their native Portugal and soon learned how to smoke and preserve meat and fish in the Indian manner.

The colonists expanded their culinary horizons. They celebrated Portuguese feast days with foods prepared from local ingredients. Native Brazilian corn-based dishes like *canjica* and *pamonha* became indispensable to the festivities of St. John's Day. Brazilian cooking was beginning to take on its own personality, one similar to that of Portugal, yet changed. The third element which truly transformed the mixture into something new would arrive in the country thirty-eight years after its discovery: the Africans.

AFRICA'S ADDITIONS
Okra, Orixa, and Dendê

From 1538 until the abolition of slavery 350 years later, the African slave would dominate the kitchens of Brazilian *casas grandes*, or big houses. Their influence on what would become the national cuisine of the country is inestimable. African slaves introduced Portuguese colonists to new tastes, among them foods cooked in palm oil, or *dendê*, the strong seasonings of the African continent, okra used as a thickener and as a vegetable, and a wide range of uses for the banana.

During the period of slavery in Brazil the presence of a Black in the kitchen was considered normal, if not indispensable. In speaking of the African influence in Brazilian cooking, it must be noted that the Portuguese colonist did not have slaves from one region of Africa alone; the vast *fazendas* (plantations) called for more and more Africans and Brazil was a melting pot for many African nations. Slaves from Angola and the Congo rubbed shoulders with others from Guinea and the Ivory Coast. Those who worshipped traditional African gods attended Catholic Mass with those who were Moslem. The diversity was enormous, with slaves from different regions being prized for different attributes. Those from the Congo and Angola were considered to be good for work in the fields, while those from Guinea, Sierra Leone, and Cape Verde, particularly the women, were thought beautiful and preferred as house servants. Slaves from the Sudanese regions of West Africa were in the majority in Bahia, while those in Rio and Pernambuco were mainly Bantu. They all brought their own tastes in food.

Starchy porridgelike mashes were one of the major components of the African diet and the *amalá*, which is Nigerian in origin, voyaged to Brazil where it retained its name, as did the Angolan *funji*. *Angu*, another of the mashes, was recorded in Brazil in 1816 and likened to a "coarse polenta" by a culinarily savvy French visitor. The variations on the starchy mash theme abound and a list of them sings with the rhythms of Africa: *bobó, vatapá, abarem, acarajé, acaça, abará,* and *carurú*. These steamed and fried African starches would form the basis for what would become one of the leading culinary traits of Bahia, the art of the *quitute,* or homemade sweet and savory dishes. Sweet porridges were also enjoyed, as were coconut candies and desserts like the Brazilian version of peanut brittle, *pé de moleque*. Soon African cooks would add local delicacies like *pamonha* and *canjica* learned from the Portuguese and native Brazilians to their menus. Many of the slave women who had a special talent for these dishes were able to escape harsher forms of toil and were allowed to sell their wares in the streets. The profits, though, went to the mistress of the house, although at times the slaves were able to retain a small portion and some even paid for their own freedom in this manner.

Africans, although they did not have chiles until the arrival of the Europeans, were known for their highly spiced foods which were seasoned using members of the *Piperaceae* (pepper) and *Zingiberaceae* (ginger) families. Their spices, like grains of paradise and melegueta peppers (called *ataré* in Yoruba) were so well known that even before Cabral happened on the territory that would become Brazil, Portuguese traders were bringing African pepper substitutes to Europe along with the true peppers of India.

The use of dried smoked fish was another African tradition that was transported to Brazil where it complemented the use of pre-served fish already extant among native Brazilians. Soon, fish smoked and dried in the manner of Senegal's *yète* and *gedj* would join the indigenous *charques*, and dried smoked shrimp would become one of the hallmarks of Afro-Bahian cooking.

One of the dishes using smoked fish was *carurú*, the oldest recorded African dish in Brazil, which was first heard of in the early seventeenth century. This stew made with leafy greens traces its origins back to Benin where it is called *obbe* and, even today, retains many of its West African ingredients: greens, vegetables, smoked fish, *dendê*, and a variety of local pepper substitutes which, in Brazil, were transformed into chiles.

Other African dishes that turn up on Brazilian menus include *aluá*, a beverage made by allowing pineapple peelings, ginger, and other ingredients to ferment; *quiabada*, a meat and okra dish; *ximxim*, a rich chicken stew prepared with ground peanuts, cashew nuts, shrimp, *dendê*, and more; and the range of *moquecas*, or stews, which are also influenced by the cooking of native Brazilians.

Perhaps the most famous of all Afro-Bahian dishes is *vatapá*, a puree of fresh and dried shrimp, onion, garlic, ginger, peanuts, cashew nuts, parsley, coconut milk, dried bread crumbs, chile, and *dendê*. The dish is so popular that singer-songwriter Dorival Caymmi, better known for his songs written for Carmen Miranda, wrote a song that gives the complete recipe in rhyming couplets.

While many dishes of African origin were retained in Brazil, virtually all of them were transformed into something different, re-created in the Brazilian mode. They were modified by the use of Brazilian ingredients or by the unavailability of African ones. However, Brazil's links to African culinary traditions were and are still quite strong. The major reason for this is the culinary component of the Candomblé religion.

In the nineteenth century, Salvador da Bahia was home to a large number of African slaves from the West African countries that would become Nigeria, Benin, and Togo. The Yoruba, Fon, and Ewe slaves from these regions brought with them their demanding gourmet gods known as *orixás*. During the final period of colonial slavery, these deities were celebrated in ceremonies that were held in remote areas. The ceremonies involved invoking the *orixás* with drum music and chanting and then venerating them with the foods that were their ritual due.

While the menus of the Big House cooks evolved and became more and more Brazilian, the menus of the Candomblé houses remained basically African, for the *orixás* would brook no changes in their ritual diets, although modifications inevitably took place. Exu, owner of the crossroads, demanded his alcohol, which in Brazil was no longer palm wine, but cachaça, the local sugarcane brandy. Xangô, the *orixá* of thunder, still craved his *amalá*, or cornmeal mush, and his consort Yansã, or Oya, the mistress of whirlwinds and the spirits, was due her ritual *acarajé*, or black-eyed pea fritters, on the first Wednesday of each month. Oxum, goddess of riches and love, was served her *xinxim*, while her sister Yemanja, goddess of motherly love and of the vast ocean, still ate the bounty of her watery regions. Omolu/Obaluaye, the physician of the poor, cleanses with popcorn. Oxalá, lord of creation, in one of his avatars, still craved true yam. Indeed the ritual year at most of Bahia's *terreiros*, or Candomblé cult houses, begins with a West African yam festival celebrating Oxalá's love for this tuber. Ogun, god of iron and all who work with it, from warriors to jewelers to taxi drivers and airline pilots, celebrates with *feijoada*, the slave meal that has become the country's national dish.

By the time that Brazil abolished slavery in 1888, the last country in the Western Hemisphere to do so, the cooking of Africa was so firmly established in Brazilian taste buds that many a Brazilian would be hard pressed to distinguish where Africa ends and Brazil begins.

NEW IMMIGRANTS

From the Middle East to Japan

Brazil attained independence from Portugal in 1822 and became its own nation. The opening of the country in the mid-nineteenth and twentieth centuries led to new waves of immigration to the country which added to the already expanding Brazilian menu. By the 1850s the new government of Brazil began to encourage European settlers to come to the land, in need of labor after the outlawing of the slave trade. The first to arrive were German and Swiss farmers who settled in the southern states of Rio Grande do Sul, Santa Catarina, and Paraná where the climate mirrored the one they had known in Europe. They brought their traditions with them and today *brau-häuser* and half-timbered chalet-style houses are common sights in Brazil's south. Italians arrived in São Paulo later in the nineteenth century and established themselves there. Their other countrymen headed for Santa Catarina where they founded the country's wine industry. In 1908 the *Kasato Maru* arrived from Japan, bringing on its decks the first of what would become 250,000 Japanese immigrants. They would settle in the São Paulo area. During the same period Syria and Lebanon sent 700,000 soon-to-be-new Brazilians, while Russia and Poland and other countries of Eastern Europe, as well as Spain, and even Portugal herself added to the cultural mosaic. Each group brought its own dishes and soon stroganoff and sushi, goulash and risotto could all be found on menus that are indeed Brazilian.

Whatever their origin, Brazilians old and new do have a common thread that runs through their history. It's their inventiveness, their ability to make do, to transform, to adapt, and to survive. Nowhere is this more visible than in their multiethnic, multifaceted cooking.

A Regional Look at Brazil's
Culinary Heritage

AMAZONAS
Giant Fish and Fabulous Fruits

The first Brazilian meal that I ever had in Brazil was in Amazonas; actually, it was in the middle of one of the narrow streams leading into the Amazon that the Brazilians call *igarapés*. Here, at the behest of the Tropical hotel in Manaus, I, along with a group of writers, had been taken to sample our first taste of Brazil. The trip was exciting, a paddlewheel boat taking us from the hotel dock to the turnoff for the tributary. Then we transferred to a small dugout canoe paddled by men who looked as though they had come straight from central casting to play Amazon prospectors. Finally we turned into a verdant cove where the sound of a small waterfall dripping onto the flat rocks played counterpoint to the music of the guitarist who greeted us as we stepped ashore. In truth, there wasn't much shore, only a small clearing where barbecue grills has been set up. Basically we stepped into the cool waters of the cove and floated along while sipping on the typically Brazilian drink that we'd just been introduced to which would become the leitmotif of that and other stays in Brazil: the caipirinha. The meal was simple, skewers of grilled shrimp and steaks of pirarucú, a flaky Amazon fish, accompanied by salads. The food was tasty, but not as wonderful as much that I would have in later days and on later trips. However, the setting was spectacular. The dappled green light filtering onto the water through the overhead network of leaves and vines, the tinkling sound of the waterfall, and the conviviality of my new friends all combined to give this meal a special Brazilian magic. How could I not come to love the food of Brazil after such an introduction?

As perfect as my introduction to the food of Brazil was, it gave me little awareness of the food of the Amazon region, perhaps some of the least-known food in all of Brazil, and certainly the most difficult to reproduce outside of the region and the country. The cooking of the Brazilian states of Pará, Roraima, Amapá, Acre, Rondônia, and Amazonas even today mirrors the cooking of the native peoples of the region. Traditionally, it depends heavily on local leaves and herbs, on corn and cassava, and on the bounty of the Amazon itself, including turtle meat and eggs and local fish, the most famous of which, the pirarucú, is known as the "bacalhau of the Amazon." Pirarucú is prepared fresh, as it was on the day that I sampled it for the first time, but it is also salted and dried, in which case it becomes the Amazonian equivalent of the sun-dried meats of the northeastern region. Other Amazon fish, like tambaqui and tucunaré, are prepared in a variety of ways. In Manaus, the rubber boom city on the banks of the Amazon, grilled tambaqui steaks are a local delicacy when served with white rice and *farofa*, toasted manioc meal. Stronger-tasting tucunaré is a main ingredient in a local stew which is flavored with chile. Today, though, many of the traditional ingredients like turtle meat are becoming rare even on Amazonian tables as increasing ecological awareness has resulted in more stringent animal preservation laws.

Belém, the major city at the mouth of the Amazon, is another spot where the cooking of the Amazon region can be sampled. There, if you can tear yourself away from the Ver-O-Paso market you can sample dishes like *tucupi tacaca*, or *pato no tucupi* (duck with tucupi). Tucupi is a condiment similar to the cassareep of Guyana. Traditionally, tucupi is prepared by mixing cassava liquid with garlic and a variety of other ingredients to get a savory sauce. In the past, women would soften the cassava by chewing it and spitting it out. Today tucupi is prepared in more hygenic ways and is a staple in many Amazonian homes. The virtual unavailability of tucupi outside of Brazil is yet another reason for the difficulty of reproducing many of the region's dishes in other areas.

Another specialty of Belém is crabs which are served in a turnoverlike pastry or simply boiled and served with a seemingly endless variety of chiles.

For desserts, the accent is frequently on local fruits, including star fruit, mangoes, cashew fruit, and others. It is impossible to walk down the streets of either Manaus or Belém and not find a kiosk selling ropes of strange fruit that are identifiable only to the locals of the region. These are prepared in sorbets, in pastes, and in the compotes that are so much a part of the traditional Brazilian dessert menu. Also on the dessert menu are dishes like *mugunzá,,* the corn and coconut pudding that is called *canjica* in the south, and crispy coconut and cassava crackers that are called *beijús.*

The star, though, of many of the dishes from the region is Brazil nuts, which are ground and added to sauces, sprinkled over soups and salads, and simply eaten roasted as an appetizer. In Brazil, they are known as *castanha-do-Pará.*

THE NORTHEAST

African Roots and Colonial Cuisine

Anytime that I mention Brazil's northeastern region, I must begin with a confession, so here goes. This is the region of the country that bewitched me. It was and still is the region that intrigues me the most with its rich history that mirrors that of the United States. It is a region that at the same time feels very much like home and yet thrills me with discoveries on each trip. In short, I'm in love with the northeast! Enough said!

The food of the northeastern region of Brazil mirrors the region's rich history. This is the region that was first settled by the Portuguese and is the seat of the country's first capital city, Salvador da Bahia do Todos os Santos. This is the region where Brazilian slavery, which began in 1538, brought an African influence to the prevailing Portuguese culture. When this met up with the traditional culture of the native Americans from regions to the north, the initial mix was complete; Brazilian culture was born.

For Brazil's culinary historians, and they are more numerous than one would at first believe, this is the region of the most unique cuisine in the entire country. This is the region that gave the country dishes such as the rich *moquecas* and savory stews that Bahian author Jorge Amado writes about so sensuously. This is the region that created a dish, *vatapá*, that songwriter Dorival Caymmi loved so much he immortalized it in a song. The northeast is a region of mythic proportions in Brazil and one of the regions that produces much that is thought of as Brazilian outside of Brazil. This is the region of the traditional tastes of Brazil: of sugar, of coconut, of chile, of *dendê*, and of cachaça.

My first meal in this region I have forgotten in a haze of pleasant memories and sensations. However, I have had so many memorable meals in the region that I have only to close my eyes and select one to be catapulted back in time and space. Perhaps the most notable meal that I ever had in the region was eaten in Bahia, in the *terreiro* of Casa Branca do Engenho Velho, one of the oldest houses of Candomblé in Brazil. Over the years I have made good friends in the white house on the hill, among the priestesses and priests who maintain the West African religion of the Yoruba people on New World shores. I have come to know them and to consider myself one of the flock and a visit to Salvador does not go by without my visiting and celebrating the dancing African gods, or *orixás*, with them.

On a recent trip, I spent the day celebrating the feast of Ogun, the *orixá* of metal. Ogun, like the other Yoruba orixás, is a demanding god. He requires devotion, veneration, prayer, and celebration with music, dance, and food. The Candomblé religion has maintained within its oral traditions the ritual recipes of the gods from West Africa and even today the dishes are prepared with what can only be described as religious fervor. Ogun's day of celebration began in the syncretized manner of Brazilian candomblé with a mass at the slaves' church on Pelourinho (the old Pillory Square of the colonial city). From there it progressed back to the *terreiro* where worshippers were served an after-church breakfast which resembled so many that I had eaten growing up: tiny cups of dark coffee—this was, after all, Brazil—accompanied by sweet rolls and cakes. However, instead of the meal taking place in the church basement to the music of an organ postlude, this was eaten to the accompaniment of African drums playing complex rhythms celebrating Ogun's glory.

As the day progressed, working up to the crescendo of the evening ceremony, preparations began again for another of Ogun's meals, this time for the black bean and smoked meat *feijoada* that is his ritual dish. The slave dish has become the national dish of his adopted country. This *feijoada* was served with great festivity at the midday meal and consumed by the votaries of the African gods who ate with gusto during the pause in the day-long ceremony. It was a simple meal, one that has its origin in a dish prepared by the slaves from the leftovers that they were given. It is a preparation that still constitutes a celebration dish for many of the people in this complex country where poverty and riches live side by side. It consisted of well-seasoned black beans and a side dish of various fatty but-oh-so-savory pieces of smoked and sun-dried pork and beef. It was also accompanied by a dish filled to the brim with sand-colored toasted manioc flour, called *farinha*, which was sprinkled on the beans and meat to give consistency and add texture. There was chile in the form of malagueta pepper for those who wanted a little heat. As we sat around the simple dining room table, I looked at my neighbors to the left and right. One was an old woman who was the granddaughter of slaves, on the other side was a youngster who had just been initiated into the religion and was still dressed in her ritual white. Each in turn spoke of the history of the religion. The elder was a living witness to the persecutions that it had survived; the younger one represented its continuation and growth at the end of the twentieth century.

Following the meal, the ceremony continued with the sacrifices of the animals that would constitute Ogun's feast and the final meal of the day. After the *matança*, the sacrifice, they were butchered ritually, with the favorite pieces of the *orixá* reserved for the meal that would be presented in his shrine. The women of the house began to cook with the same multigenerational fervor that goes on in American kitchens, at church suppers, and Thanksgiving family dinners. Each person had a job and, as it was for ritual purposes, each made sure that her work was done well. Cooking for the gods is tedious and time-consuming, as no food processors or work savers are allowed in the *terreiro* kitchens. Even the cooking itself is done in the traditional manner, over wood-burning fires, so as not to offend the tastes of the gourmet gods.

The third and final part of the ceremony is the part that is witnessed by many visitors to the Candomblé houses. It is even open to the public and can be seen by any respectful visitor to Bahia. However, those watching the votaries of the *orixás* dance in their brightly colored skirts and turbans and ropes of glass bead necklaces cannot know of the beauty of the total day with the *orixás* that few suspect, even fewer see. If they do, they are among the fortunate: those who are invited to partake of the meal that is served in the pause in the evening ceremony are those who have truly eaten the food of the gods.

This food is at the base of much of the cooking of Bahia and the northeast. In fact, one culinary historian, Luis da Camara Cascudo, claims that the food of the northeast can actually be divided into two regions, that of Bahia, and that of the rest of the region. Whatever the chosen breakdown, the African *orixás* and their dishes are the origin of many of the region's best-known dishes such as *vatapá*, *efo*, *caruru*, *ximxim*, and others. The cooking of Bahia and the northeast is also known for being dependent on oral tradition. Only recently have recipes begun to be written down. For a good cook from the region, the most important thing to have in her culinary arsenal is *"um boa mão,"* a good hand, or the ability to season well and judge the amounts of oil, coconut milk, and chile necessary in each dish. No recipe can ever do that because of the differences in quality and in taste of these very necessary ingredients.

In the other regions of the northeast, food is much simpler than it is in Bahia. Markets in the interior offer a variety of beans and types of cassava meal, and even fresh vegetables—though they don't make frequent solo appearances on the table—and the number of different tropical fruits is astounding. However, tomatoes usually appear as a garnish and the meal is more often than not prepared from sun-dried meat prepared from either goat or ox, or fish, with the addition of such vegetable and herbal staples as ginger, garlic, coriander, tomatoes, dried smoked shrimp, okra, coconut milk, and, in the region around Bahia, *dendê*, or palm oil. Chile is often used in the dishes of this region, with the most popular being the *pimenta malagueta*, which is similar to the tabasco chile, and the *pimenta do cheiro*, which is like the habanero. In the coastal areas, fish in all its variety reigns supreme on the menu.

Throughout the region, there are also local specialties. Lobster, crab, and shrimp are grilled and fresh fish is fried or stewed and served in the beachfront restaurants in Fortaleza in the state of

Ceará, while São Luis in the state of Maranhão is known for its giant shrimp that are usually served fried. As the country's sugarcane growing region, the northeast is also known as the home of cachaça and near Vitória de Santo Antão, home of Pitú, the most popular brand of cachaça in the northeast, visitors can watch the sugarcane brandy being made and sample the product.

RIO AND SÃO PAULO
Cariocas and Caipirinhas

Brazil's supercosmopolitan cities, Rio and São Paulo, are anomalies in the study of the national food. They have been so influenced by tourism and by the tastes of the rich that it is only by staying a while and scratching the surface that the visitor can see what the food is really like. In addition to this, the local foods typical of the region have given way to imported dishes like pizza and stroganoff and even sushi.

Rio is a casual city, one where for many men wearing a shirt and tie signals either a funeral to attend or serious business being transacted. This casual attitude is also seen in Rio's restaurants where diners can appear jacketless in most. Perhaps the meal most typical of Rio de Janeiro is a Saturday *feijoada,* for it is a meal that expresses both the city's basic meat-and-potatoes attitude toward food and celebrates its many beaches at the same time. From Copacabana to Leblon and beyond, the Rio shore is lined with hotels and restaurants with ocean views. While these restaurants are pleasant enough on any given day of the week, they truly come to life on Saturday when the Cariocas (natives of Rio) celebrate their love of food, flesh, and the beach. The restaurants fill at lunchtime and reservations are sometimes necessary to secure a good seat by the window. *Feijoada* is a Saturday institution for Cariocas because it is impossible to have such a heavy meal and then expect to do anything except indulge in an indolent afternoon or, better yet, a long nap. The only thing better than a *feijoada* in one of Rio's restaurants is one in a friend's home and then the treat is even better. Of necessity, because of the enormous quantities of food served, a Rio *feijoada* is a long, leisurely affair; the afternoon passes in conviviality and friendly discussion. The same restaurants are transformed in the evening and frequently serve buffets where fish and shellfish are the drawing cards. Then, with the dark rocks of the bay looming out of the night and the twinkling of the lights of the shoreline, they take on another aspect, becoming more sophisticated dining spots.

Another type of restaurant that is one of the delights of Rio is the *churrascaria,* a restaurant specializing in gaucho-style barbecue. These serve a variety of meats that have been marinated in special sauces and are served either to order or in the *rodízio* style where waiters parade around in a seemingly endless ballet carrying sword-like skewers of meat which they slice on each plate according to the diner's taste. Vegetables and salads are found at many *churrascarias* and some even have salad bars.

But this is only the tip of Rio's dining iceberg. Cariocas have a wide range of fresh produce at their very doorsteps, thanks to the numerous local neighborhood markets that spring up around the city on different days of the week. Here Cariocas can find fresh fish brought almost to their kitchens by vendors such as the Cosme and Damian Flying Fish Market, which proudly serves its customers fish still dripping with seawater from a shop counter in the side of a panel truck. Vendors vie with each other in the artistic display of their wares and fruit and vegetable vendors seem to have a special knack for arranging their produce by hue. Cariocas revel in these markets and have even coined a special word, *xepa,* to describe the foods that are purchased in the final minutes before the market closes (the best time to get a bargain on the sometimes less-than-perfect items that remain).

Rio's informality is easily contrasted with the businesslike sophistication of São Paulo, Brazil's fastest growing and most prosperous city to the south. São Paulo is known throughout Brazil for the excellence of its restaurants. No other city in Brazil offers the variety of restaurants that São Paulo does. Restaurant choices range from Italian trattorias like the Jardim de Napoli and Massimo's to French, like the Largo do Arouche and La Cuisine du Soleil in the Maksoud Plaza Hotel. But there are also ethnic foods that would seem unusual to one who has not studied Brazil's history of immigration in this century. There are beer halls like the Bismarck and Konstanz which serve German wurst and beers in good imitation of the best that Bavaria can offer. Then there are the Japanese restaurants of the Liberdade district which serve sushi, tempura, and teriyaki prepared to the tastes of the Japanese population of São Paulo which is the largest population of Japanese outside of Japan!

My São Paulo food memories are of a dinner with my friend Nair de Carvalho in a Japanese restaurant where I had *shabu shabu*, a winter dish of sliced beef and vegetables cooked at the table in a broth. The meal was accompanied by warmed sake and Japanese beer and, if I closed my eyes, I could easily believe that I was in Tokyo or Osaka and not São Paulo, such is the magic of the city's Japanese food.

At home, Paulista cooks are also adventurous and several Brazilian specialties owe their origin to their inventiveness. Dishes like *camarões a paulista*—grilled shrimp—and *cuscuz brasileiro*—a savory steamed cornmeal porridge—are from this region, where the influence of the Portuguese colonists can be seen in the use of olive oil and garlic. This, though, is a region that brings variety to the Brazilian menu; one where nouvelle cuisine dishes by Troisgros appear on restaurant menus alongside traditional food from Japan, Italy, Germany, Russia, and the Middle East.

Finally, São Paulo is also known as the capital of Brazilian coffee. Many Paulista fortunes from the beginning of this century were made from the beverage which Paulistas like to drink, as they put it, "black as the night, strong as love, sweet as a kiss, and hot as hell!"

THE CENTRAL HEARTLAND
King Bean's Paradise

The central regions of Brazil—the states of Goiás and Minas Gerais, and Espírito Santo—are marked in matters culinary by their love of beans. *Tutu a mineira*, the mashed beans with kale and pork chop dish from Minas Gerais, is perhaps the best example of the cooking of this region where in places it is not unusual for people to eat as many as five meals a day! Following a love of beans, the next favorites on the culinary hit parade are the starchy mashes known as *pirão* which rival rice in popularity.

The state of Minas Gerais has been called Brazil's heart by some writers. Indeed, while not located in the geographic center of the country (that honor goes to the neighboring state of Goiás), it boasts some of the country's best preserved historical monuments and much of the country's mineral wealth. In fact, the name of the state means "general mines" in Portuguese in reference to the mines that furnished the gold and diamonds that were the wealth of the region in the eighteenth century. Mineros are known as ardent preservationists and Ouro Prêto, the center of the eighteenth century gold rush, has been transformed into a veritable living museum of Brazilian baroque art.

Mineros are also preservationists in matters of cooking. They have preserved their large wood-burning ovens called *fogão de lenha* in which they still prepare a number of their dishes. Pork is king in Minas Gerais and is served in a variety of ways, from roasted in wood-burning ovens to prepared in a wide range of sausages, or lingüiças, and bacons. Coming in second as a favorite meat is chicken, which is traditionally served in a dark blood sauce (*galinha ao molho pardo*) or with okra. Mineros are not great milk drinkers, so the milk that is produced from their numerous herds is made into cheese. Indeed, the cheeses of the region are famous throughout Brazil and are important ingredients in the biscuits and crackers for which the region is also renowned.

Neighboring Goiás is perhaps best known as the state which includes the Distrito Federal, the federal district where the capital, Brasília, is located. Begun by president Juscelino Kubitschek in 1956 and designed by architect Oscar Niemeyer, the city surges from the red dust and twisted scrub trees like a mirage. Built on a plan that has been alternately described as an airplane and a cross, the city is impressive, but its remoteness and lack of history have made it a place that many Brazilians deride. (They are proud of its existence and its survival, but living there is not something they would consider.) The Carioca government workers who were given the choice of moving to Brasília or losing their jobs, the staffs of many of the embassies, and indeed any who can afford it, flee the city on weekends, heeding Rio's siren song or succumbing to the lure of Bahia.

Needless to add, I arrived in Brasília on one of those weekends for my first and last trip to the country's capital. The city was impressive indeed, and in its Saturday night deserted state seemed as though it were an empty movie set designed by a modern Cecil B. deMille. This illusion was rapidly banished as I journeyed with friends to the residential wings where the people live and play. There, samba music blared from open club doorways, restaurants were filled with dining patrons, and discotheques lured the young with their driving beat. We found a restaurant and ordered what everyone else seemed to be having: a steak and salad. It was fine, well-cooked and tasty, but far from the best that I'd had in Brazil.

Brasília is not a city for diners. Restaurants are good, but not spectacular and local specialties are found only occasionally. Like its neighbors in Minas Gerais to the east, the inhabitants of Goiás cook in traditional wood-burning ovens and like them they appreciate pork and the fish that run abundantly in local rivers. The region is also known for its local wine prepared from a small red fruit called catuabá.

One thing, though, that is typical of the cooking of Goiás and indeed that I was able to sample on my night of dining in Brasília, is the region's abundant use of chile. This state is a chile lover's dream, with chiles in all sizes and shapes, from the traditional Brazilian malagueta to the fiery hot varieties of habanero called *pimenta do cheiro*. They appear in hot sauces and condiments on virtually all of the region's tables and are reason enough for any chile lover to spend some time in Goiás.

In Espírito Santo, on the coast, cooking is influenced by the African practices of Bahia to the north and of the state of Rio de Janeiro to the south. The Capixabas, as the natives are called, have their own versions of many dishes that are familiar in other regions, like *cozidos*—stews—and *feijoadas*. The telltale orange hue of Bahia's *dendê*, or palm oil, is replaced in some dishes from the region by a homemade annatto oil called *oleo de urucum*.

My friend Erminha Apolinario is a Capixaba who lives in New York and she adeptly reproduces the food of her region in northern kitchens. Through her, I have learned how to enjoy dishes like the Capixaba versions of *mugunzá*—a corn and coconut porridge—and *moqueca* and a *feijoada* that the folk from Vitória prepare with pink beans instead of the black ones typical of Rio.

BIG COUNTRY: THE FAR WEST

Wild Game and the Last Frontier

More than any other section of Brazil, this region has the feeling of the last frontier. The region is sparsely populated. As recently as the 1960s there were few paved roads in the area and it was seen as one of opportunity for many of the drought-fleeing migrants from the northeast and others leaving the overpopulated south. Yet the region is one of the fastest growing in Brazil. It can all be seen in the names of the two states that make up this section: Mato Grosso and Mato Grosso do Sul, which can be translated as Big Country and Southern Big Country.

Adventurers who journeyed to the region, and I admit that I have not, will find that meat is the basis of the diet. Up until recent measures were taken to protect local wildlife, animals like capivaras, the world's largest rodent that looks for all the world like a giant guinea pig, horny shelled armadillos, and other local fauna found their way from hunters' game bags to local tables.

Anyone who visits Brazil's wildlife preserve in the region known as the Pantanal which consists of forty thousand square miles on the border between Mato Grosso and Mato Grosso do Sul will understand the richness of the region. Those who sign on for sport fishing trips will know why fish is the other popular local food, with fish like pintados and dourado abounding in local rivers. According to naturalists, there are over 350 varieties of fish in local waters.

THE DEEP SOUTH

Weinstuben and Trattoria and the Beefeater's Paradise

The south of Brazil seems to be a country distinct from the north and west. Here, in the blink of an eye, it is possible to think you're in Europe. The climate is one of the reasons, as here Brazil has a temperate climate not unlike that of Europe. Here, too, the people are different and blue-eyed blonds are more frequently found than in the north. African influence and that of the native Brazilians are limited, not to say nonexistent.

People here hark back to their roots in Germany or Italy and much of the architecture, many of the festivals, and most of the food springs from these roots as well. Blumenau in Santa Catarina is the unlikely location of the largest Oktoberfest in South America, one which annually attracts crowds of almost a million visitors. Rio Grande do Sul is the home of Brazil's thriving wine industry and accounts for 90 percent of the country's wine production. Cities hold grape, champagne, and wine festivals almost year-round, with dancing and sampling that would be right at home in Tuscany.

The Germans and Italians who arrived in this region immigrated to Brazil in the nineteenth century following upheavals in Europe. They established their own enclaves and maintained customs and traditions much as they had in their European homes. A recent Brazilian soap opera was set in this region and each time that it was on the television, I marveled that this too was Brazil. In fact, the only non-German element in the soap opera was the language in which it was acted: Portuguese. This too is a recent development, as for many years natives of these southern states stuck determinedly to their German or Italian. It was only with the advent of World War II, when the population of this region largely favored the Axis powers, that the government put its foot down and insisted on instruction in Portuguese in the schools and adopted other means of assimilating the inhabitants into the Brazilian population at large.

Along with their European heritage, the states of Paraná, Rio Grande do Sul, and Santa Catarina are also the breadbasket of Brazil. Paraná is home to coffee plantations, while Rio Grande do Sul is the location of the country's largest cattle farms and its leading grain producers. Indeed, the south can be divided into two distinct culinary traditions: those of its Italian and German immigrants and those of the gauchos. *Biergärten* are rife in the area near Novo Petropolis, one city that celebrates the area's German heritage. Diners can sample locally made wurst and salamis, a well as risottos and stroganoffs, and drink some of the excellent local wines. The food is good and even excellent in some places, but there is little that is truly Brazilian.

The wines of the region are another matter, for the vintages of the coastal mountains of the state of Rio Grande do Sul have steadily improved since the early Italian immigrants started producing wines in the region in the 1880s. Today, the wine-producing areas center around the towns of Caxias do Sul, Garibaldi, and Bento Gonçalves, the area's "capital."

Maison Forestier, one of Brazil's top producers of table wines, is owned by Seagram's and is continually at work on upgrading their product. Experts predict that one day Brazilian wines, particularly the whites, will rival those of neighboring Chile and Argentina for leadership in South America. Brazil also produces its own champagne. The French company Moët-Chandon which has spearheaded research in the growing of champagne grapes in regions outside of the Champagne region owns one of the vineyards. The reds lag in third place, but several excellent table wines can be found locally.

Wurst, risottos, and wines, though, are only half the tale of the cooking of Brazil's Deep South. The other half is of cowboys who roam the pampas wearing baggy pantaloon trousers, hand-tooled leather belts and boots, and flat hats, for this is also the land of the gauchos. Indeed, many connect the gaucho life-style only with neighboring Argentina, when Brazil, in fact, has its own pampas in Rio Grande do Sul and, yes, its own gauchos. They have contributed one of their traditional dishes to the country's culinary lexicon: the *churrasco.*

This gaucho barbecue has captured the minds and taste buds of the entire country and *churrascarias*—restaurants in which it is served—can be found throughout the country, from Porto Alegre to Belém, Rio de Janeiro to Brasília. Ironically, *churrasco,* according to some culinary historians, was not created by gauchos, for beef cattle, which were imported into Brazil from the Cape Verde Islands, only arrived in the region from the north in 1780. However, when the cattle arrived they thrived on what is some of the best pasture land in the country. It was the arrival of the cattle and their fortuitous adaptation to the climate that led to the local taste for cooked fresh meat in the place of the more typical smoked or sun-dried meat so widely eaten in the region.

Whatever the origin of the *churrasco,* it is undeniable that today the gauchos are known throughout the country as experts in the art of preparing the barbecued meats and the typical sauce, called *molho campanha,* that accompanies them. Along with the consumption of vast quantities of barbecued meat, gaucho mythology calls for the drinking of maté, a caffeine-laden tea which is traditionally sipped through a silver straw called a *bomba* from a silver-decorated gourd called a *chimarrão.*

✿   ✿   ✿

Brazil has been called a continent with its colonies inside it. The historical, cultural, and culinary diversity of the country's regions is enormous. Indeed, Brazil seems to offer within its 3,286,488 square miles something for almost everyone, from the densely populated Altantic beachfront playgrounds of Rio to the unspoiled coastal areas of Jericoacoara in the northeast, from the Amazonian rain forest to the high rises of São Paulo, from the thundering of Iguaçu Falls to the calm of the Pantanal, and from the history of Salvador da Bahia and Ouro Prêto to the modernity of Brasília.

Brazilian Market Basket

For me one of the most agreeable parts of the preparation of any meal is the shopping. I enjoy learning how to use new ingredients and finding new additions to my larder. I also love to experiment with new tastes. It follows then that a good part of the fun of cooking Brazilian is the wide variety of ingredients that are used. The vast country can boast that its cuisine calls into play ingredients that are African, European, Asian, native American, Middle Eastern, and, naturally, Brazilian. For this reason, some of the ingredients called for in the recipes that will follow will be unfamiliar, although most can be found relatively easily on a shelf in your local supermarket which you may not normally search. Alternately, the few more specialized ingredients can be found in either specialty shops in your hometown, or in ethnic neighborhoods. Finally, truly hard to obtain ingredients can be ordered from the mail-order sources listed in the back of the book. The following listing will show you how to shop for some of the less well known ingredients that are called for in some of the recipes. Don't panic. When an ingredient is really difficult to find, I've tried to offer suggestions for more readily available substitutes.

A LISTING OF UTENSILS,
INGREDIENTS, AND DISHES

ABACATE (*Persea gratissima*) AVOCADO

This fruit of the avocado tree is also known as vegetable butter or midshipman's butter. In Brazil the avocado is used less frequently in salads than in the Caribbean or Mexico. Instead, it finds its way into juices and desserts like *Sorvete de Abacate* (page 235). Several types of avocado are available year-round in supermarkets in North America. When purchas· ıg avocados, be sure to select ripe ones that give slightly to the touch but are still firm. Avocados that are too soft may have dark overripe spots when cut open.

ABACAXI (*Ananas sativus*) PINEAPPLE

This cultivated bromeliad is much appreciated in Brazil where it turns up in everything from salads like *Salada de Galinha e Abacaxi* (page 190) to roasted as an accompaniment for meats such as *Abacaxi Assado* (page 164). Its juice is savored fresh or added to cachaça to produce batidas (see pages 246–248). Even the peel is used, boiled with water, ginger, and spices and allowed to ferment until it becomes *aluá,* an Afro-Brazilian drink similar to many West African beverages.

Brazil is favored with several types of pineapple, including wild ones. Here pineapples are available in supermarkets and at green-grocers year-round. One test for ripeness is to lightly tug on one of the green leaves. If it comes off and if the fruit yields slightly to the touch and smells ripe, you've got a winner.

ABÓBORA (*Cucurbita* species)
CALABAZA OR WEST INDIAN COOKING PUMPKIN

Pumpkin in Brazil turns up in a variety of ways. It is a vegetable that appears in stews and as purees (page 140) and even turns up sugared on the dessert table (pages 216, 220). The Brazilian pumpkin, though, is not the Halloween jack-o'-lantern pumpkin; it is firmer. In the United States, it is called calabaza, or West Indian cooking pumpkin. The Portuguese brought them to Brazil from Guinea in West Africa in the first half of the sixteenth century. As they grow quite large, you can usually find them sold by the piece in Caribbean and Latin American markets. Look for unblemished pieces. If purchased whole, they can be kept for several months in a cool, dry place. In pieces, they will keep only a few days in the refrigerator. If this type of pumpkin cannot be found, substitute Hubbard or butternut squash in preference to the American pumpkin.

ACHIOTE. See *Urucu*

AGRIÃO (*Nasturtium palustre*) WATERCRESS
When most North Americans think of watercress, they think of neatly cut tea sandwiches and garnishes on restaurant plates. In Brazil, however, bity watercress turns up frequently in salads (page 127) where it mixes with fresh tomatoes and tart onions.

When shopping for watercress, which is readily available, look for deep green unblemished leaves and stems that have not become pulpy.

A plant in the northeastern state of Pará, called *agrião do Pará* (*Spilanthes oleracea*), is similar to chicory. It is mixed with ground fish, shrimp and other ingredients and is a main ingredient in tucupi (see page 52).

AIPIM (*Manihot* species) CASSAVA, MANIOC
This relative of the poinsettia was and is one of the staffs of life for the native Indians who dwelt in the Brazilian forests. There are several varieties of this tuber which is about ten inches long and two inches in diameter. This versatile root vegetable produces everything from tapioca to the cassava meal that is readily available in Latin American grocery stores. In Brazil it is frequently used in purees and starchy mashes called *pirões* that accompany stews, and in desserts and sweets. Its liquid is the basis for the Amazon's tucupi and it turns up batter-fried in São Paulo's Japanese tempuras. It also appears on virtually every Brazilian table as *farinha* (toasted flour which is used to thicken and add texture to soups and stews) and as a wide variety of *farofas* (pages 104–108), toasted cassava meal to which a variety of ingredients can be added.

The bitter cassava variety (*Manihot esculenta*) is not available in northern markets for it must be cooked at length to rid it of its prussic acid content. The sweet variety (*Manihot aipi* or *Manihot dulcis*) is easily found in Latin and West Indian markets. It should be purchased when the skin is a shiny dark brown and the flesh is white and hard to the touch.

While fresh cassava is used in Brazil, the recipes selected for this book usually call for the more readily available cassava meal, which is the flour processed from the starchy tuber. It is available in Hispanic markets and specialty food stores and will keep for six months or longer in a sealed container.

AMENDOIM (Arachis hypogaea) PEANUTS

Peanuts come into their own in Brazilian cooking where they are found used in everything from main dishes, like Bahia's *Ximxim de Galinha* (page 184) where they thicken and add texture, to beverages like the *Batida de Amendoim* (page 248). They also appear roasted as snacks along with drinks and in desserts like *Paçoca* (page 229) and *Pé-de-Moleque* (page 230).

Brazilians usually purchase their peanuts raw and roast them themselves. Raw peanuts can be found at greengrocers or in health food stores. They can be toasted by drizzling them with oil and placing them in a shallow baking dish in a 350°F oven and checking frequently until they are brown. For additional taste, roast them until they have a deep brown hue. They then can be processed into butters or used in brittles, drinks, or desserts as you wish.

ANISE. See Erva Doce

ANNATTO. See Urucu

ARROZ (Oryza sativa) RICE

Along with black beans, rice makes frequent appearances on the Brazilian table. Rice can be served plain with butter and salt, or in a variety of ways with additions of everything from garlic, minced onions, and *carne seca*, or bacon, which makes it almost a main dish (page 148) to sugar and coconut milk which transforms it into a dessert.

In Brazil, rice is usually purchased by the pound and much time is spent picking out the impurities. Brazilian rice is usually long grain and cooked until every grain stands by itself. (Unless, of course, you're in the south where the Italian love for risottos takes over.) Select the rice that you like best and serve it light and fluffy.

Basic Rice

───── ◆ ─────

MAKES 6 TO 8 SERVINGS

Well-prepared white rice is something that is simply a given in most Brazilian kitchens. Each grain should stand by itself. Here's how.

3½ cups water

1½ cups long-grain rice

1 teaspoon salt

1 tablespoon unsalted butter

Bring the water to a boil in a saucepan over medium heat. Stir in the rice, salt, and butter. Cover, reduce the heat to low, and simmer for about 20 minutes. Remove the saucepan from the heat and allow it to stand for five minutes, or until the remaining water has been absorbed. Fluff with a fork and serve hot.

AVOCADO. See *Abacate*

BACALHAU DRIED CODFISH
The love of dried codfish comes to Brazil straight from the Portuguese. It was until recently a dish of the poor. However, the price of *bacalhau* has risen and many of the poor can no longer afford it. *Bacalhau* appears in a variety of ways on the Brazilian table, reconstituted and stewed in coconut milk in Bahia and in a traditional Portuguese stew with tomatoes and onions in much of the south of the country.

Bacalhau is available in Portuguese markets and in vegetable markets in West Indian neighborhoods. When selecting *bacalhau*, look for pieces that have firm white flesh; yellow flesh indicates age. Before preparing it, you must reconstitute the fish by soaking it to remove the salt.

An ingredient in many Brazilian dishes, *bacalhau* is easily resconstituted.

Soak the salted codfish in cold water overnight. The following day, drain the fish, place it in a saucepan, and cover with fresh cold water. Bring the water to a boil and simmer the fish over medium-low heat for 15 minutes, or until tender. Drain, then skin and flake the fish.

If you're pressed for time or overnight soaking is simply too much trouble, place the salted fish in a pan, cover it with fresh cold water, and bring it quickly to a boil. Then simmer it for 15 minutes, drain the fish, skin it, and flake it. (Some people boil the fish in milk and claim that it enhances the flavor.)

BACALHAU BRASILEIRO DRIED LOCAL FISH

As salted codfish has become increasingly expensive over the years, resourceful Brazilians have begun to prepare their own salted fish from the fish taken from local waters. These are known as *bacalhau brasileiro* or locally as *bacalhau do pobre* (poor folks' *bacalhau*).

BANANA (*Musa* species) BANANAS

The banana as we know it arrived in Brazil from Africa, although there was already a local variety known as a *pacova*. In the early years, they were eaten with wine, sugar, and cinnamon. During the period of slavery, they were prized because roasted green ones were thought to provide "almost the sustenance of bread," according to Luís de Camara Cascudo. The same culinary historian states that the banana is the most popular of all of the adopted Brazilian fruits. There are numerous varieties of bananas grown in Brazil, ranging from the plantains, or large cooking ones, to small sweet ones eaten as snacks by schoolchildren. They are used in a variety of ways in Brazilian cooking, boiled and mashed into purees, roasted and ground into flour, blended into drinks, baked, fried, and simply eaten raw.

More and more different types of bananas are finding their way into North American greengrocers and supermarkets. Today green bananas and plantains are available in many urban neighborhoods and at times even the small finger bananas can be found. Bananas should be purchased when their skins are unblemished and they are firm to the touch. They should never be refrigerated. Plantains can be used in various stages of ripeness, from green to black, but you must know what stage you want, as they cannot be used interchangeably because as bananas and plantains ripen, their starch is transformed into sugar.

Folha de banana, or banana leaves, also get into the act and are a necessary item for the preparation of such Bahian specialties as *abará* and *acaçá* which are steamed in them. They are available occasionally in markets in Latin American neighborhoods. If you find them, wash them well, soak them to soften them, and then cut into pieces the necessary size. There is no substitute for banana leaves.

BEANS. See *Feijão*

BLACK PEPPER. See *Pimenta-do-Reino*

BRAZIL NUT. See *Castanha-do-Pará*

CACHAÇA BRAZILIAN SUGARCANE BRANDY
One treatise on food in Brazil calls this sugarcane brandy "the principal item responsible for the evils of alcoholism in the rural population." This liquor, which is similar in taste, if not potency, to the raw white rums of Haiti and to the white lightnings of the southern United States, is used to mix many of the typical Brazilian drinks called batidas and caipirinhas.

There are many brands of cachaça throughout the country and numerous local names for the beverage, many of them quite colorful like *abrideira* (opener) which applies to the liquor and to all aperitifs, and *mata-bicho* (animal killer). (Drinking before meals is sometimes referred to as "killing the animal"—*matar o bicho*.)

Today cachaça is enjoying a vogue with the middle and upper classes where it used to be derided as the drink of the poor. People are serving estate-bottled cachaças in cut-glass decanters and even preparing their own flavored ones from old family recipes.

CAJU (*Anacardium occidentale*) CASHEW

This fruit has two distinct parts: the tart-tasting red-orange fruit itself and the one we know in the United States, the crescent-shaped nut that hangs from the end of the fruit. The fruit is eaten raw in Brazil and is transformed into batidas, fruit salads, and compotes. It is not available in the United States and there is no substitute.

The nut, known in Portuguese as *castanha do caju,* is roasted and eaten as s snack, pulverized and added to dishes like Bahia's *Xinxim de Galinha* (page 184) and *Carurú* (page 200), and in candies and desserts like some varieties of *Paçoca* and *Pé-de-Moleque.* Cashew nuts are readily available in the United States. If possible, obtain them raw and roast them yourself as you would roast peanuts (see page 30).

CAMARÃO SHRIMP

In Brazil three are several varieties of shrimp available, ranging in size from the tiny ones that occasionally turn up called *cisco,* to the large freshwater ones similar to crayfish called *pitú,* which is also the brand name of a popular cachaça. Shrimp turn up in all sorts of dishes in the coastal regions, most particularly as *Espetinhos de Camarão* (page 202) or as *Camarões a Paulista* (page 203).

Shrimp should be purchased when they are fresh (know your fishmonger) and be prepared immediately. They can be boiled in advance and then frozen to await the remaining preparations. If so, peel and devein them first and do not keep the shrimp for more than a few weeks.

To precook shrimp for use in salads and in sauces, remove the shells by pressing on them with your fingers; they will slide off. Then, with the point of a knife, remove the dark vein from the outside curve of the body. This is best done under cold running water. When finished, place the shrimp in a saucepan with enough water to cover. Add 2 teaspoons of salt per pound of shrimp and thyme and fresh peppercorns for flavor, cover, and bring the water to a boil. Cook for 2 to 4 minutes. Drain and use.

CAMARÃO SECO DRIED SHRIMP

This is a taste that Bahia residents got from West Africa. The shrimp in this case are dried and occasionally smoked, which gives them a distinctive odor that is quite strong and unpleasant to some. These shrimp are usually pulverized and added to Afro-Bahian dishes like *Ximxim de Galinha* (page 184) and *Carurú* (page 200) to add flavor and consistency. If using the large ones whole, they should be shelled prior to use. Dried smoked shrimp can be found in Chinese supermarkets, but if you are fortunate enough to find the larger, stronger-tasting West African types, you will be able to truly duplicate the taste of Bahia.

CANELA (*Cinnamomum zeylanicum*) CINNAMON

This seasoning is made from the dried inner bark of the cinnamon tree. The spice is used to season desserts and some main dishes. It is thought to stimulate digestion.

When using cinnamon, or any spice in fact, always try to get the whole form, as the powdered versions are frequently adulterated with other less-expensive ingredients. Cinnamon quills (sticks) are readily available and can be pulverized in a spice or coffee grinder that you have reserved for that purpose.

CARANGUEJO MANGROVE CRABS

This edible crustacean is found more frequently on Brazilian menus than its sea-inhabiting cousin the *siri* (see page 51). There are several Brazilian types which appear on local tables in many forms. The simplest is boiled in salted water and served with slices of lemon. Others call for a variety of sauces. These crabs are difficult to find in North America; you can substitute fresh or lump crabmeat, but you will not have quite the same delicate taste.

CARNE DEFUMADO SMOKED MEAT

This meat is distinguished from *carne seca* (see below) in that it is smoked as well as dried.

CARNE DE SOL. See *Carne Seca*

CARNE SECA DRIED MEAT

This is a sun-dried meat that is typically used in many Brazilian dishes, notably *Feijoada* (page 171) and *Arroz de Hauça* (page 148). The meat is prepared by salting it and leaving it in the sun and the wind to dry thoroughly. *Carne seca* can be prepared from various types of meat, from domestic cattle to buffalo. This meat, which is also known as *charque* or *carne de sol,* is quite tough, but savory, with a distinctive taste that has no substitute.

Carne seca is occasionally available in Brazilian neighborhoods. If found, it must be desalted before using by soaking it in several changes of water. If it cannot be found, slab bacon can be substituted, but the taste is definitely not the same.

CASHEW. See *Caju*

CASSAVA. See *Aipim*

CASTANHA DO CAJU. See *Caju*

CASTANHA-DO-PARÁ

(*Lecitidacea amazonica, Bertholletia excelsa*) BRAZIL NUT

These are the seeds of the plant which grow in large pods, with each nut occupying a separate segment. The seeds, or nuts to us, are also known to some as vegetable meat for they contain carbohydrates, fats, albumins, and vitamins A and B, among other elements. There are tales of lost hunters surviving solely on Brazil nuts until they were rescued.

In the Amazon region the nuts are crushed to yield a milk which is added to porridges. In other parts of the country, they are roasted and nibbled as snacks with aperitifs or find their way into desserts and candies.

Brazil nuts are readily available in North America. As with all nuts, purchase them raw in the shell, crack them, and roast them yourself if possible (see page 30).

CHARQUE. See *Carne Seca*

CHARQUE DE PEIXE. See *Bacalhau Brasileiro*

CHAYOTE. See *Xuxu*

CHOURIÇO PORTUGUESE BLOOD SAUSAGE

In Brazil these sausages are generally prepared locally or even at home. Natural casings are used to hold a stuffing of pork, herbs, and spices. Technically, chouriços include cooked animal blood. They are sometimes also known as morcela. There are an infinite variety of chouriços. (See also Lingüiça.)

Chouriços can be found in Portuguese neighborhoods. If not, chorizo, the Spanish variation, is available fairly readily at stores in Latin American neighborhoods and in many supermarkets.

CLOVE. See *Cravo-da-índia*

COCO (Cocos nucifera) COCONUT

In Brazil the word *coco* applies to the fruit of all of the varieties of coconut palm. Coconut milk and grated fresh coconut are the most frequently used items from this versatile plant. The coconut water, though, taken from green coconuts has great popularity in the beach areas of the country. There is also coconut oil, which is the cooking oil of choice in some parts of the country.

In Bahia, in the northeast, coconut is considered to be one of the region's holy trinity of ingredients, along with *dendê*, or palm oil (see page 39), and malagueta pepper (see page 48). There it appears in main dishes like *moquecas* (page 197), in desserts like *Cocadas* (pages 214–216) and mixed with cachaça in a variety of drinks.

Coconuts are readily available in the United States. When selecting coconuts in the supermarket, shake them well to make sure they are full of water. (They should slosh.)

The liquid that comes out of the coconut when it is opened is coconut water. Coconut milk must be prepared. Brazilians use and prepare two types of coconut milks, thick and thin. The first thing to do is open the coconut. There are several methods for this. Some people prefer to open the coconut by whacking it on a cement floor. This is too difficult and all too often ends in coconut puree and coconut water on the walls. I prefer to heat the coconut by leaving it under hot running water or placing it in a 350°F oven for ten minutes. The coconut will develop fault lines. Remove the coconut from the oven and, holding it in a cloth (it will be hot!) over a large bowl, hit it along the fault lines with a hammer or heavy mallet. The coconut will open. Reserve the liquid, remove the meat from the coconut shell, and take off the brown outer pieces with a paring knife. The coconut is now ready. To grate coconut, use either a hand grater or food processor and proceed as usual.

TO PREPARE THICK COCONUT MILK

Grate the coconut, then wrap it in cheesecloth and pour ½ cup warm water over it while holding it over a bowl. Squeeze the liquid from the coconut into the bowl. This is thick coconut milk. You should get about ¾ cup from each coconut.

TO PREPARE THIN COCONUT MILK

Prepare the thick coconut milk as instructed above, then add the reserved coconut water and grated coconut residue from the thick coconut milk. It's time-consuming, but it's the only way that you'll end up with a truly Brazilian taste. If you're stuck, and only if you're stuck, unsweetened desiccated coconut can be substituted. Alternately, coconut milk can be purchased in bottles from specialty stores.

CODFISH. See *Bacalhau*

COENTRO (*Coriandrum sativum*) FRESH CORIANDER OR CILANTRO
The flat green leaves of the coriander plant are one of the major herbal seasonings in Brazilian cooking. They appear in dishes like *moquecas* (page 197) and *ensopados* (page 206) and turn up in sauces like *Molho Brasileiro* (page 96).

Leaf coriander can be found easily at greengrocers and in supermarkets. Look for leaves that are unblemished and deep green.

CORN. See *Milho*

COUVE (*Brassica oleracea*) KALE

The love of this leafy green vegetable would seem to be another Brazilian inheritance from the Portuguese. It turns up in strips in soups like *Canja* (page 113) and is the traditional accompaniment to *Feijoada* (page 171) and *Tutu a Mineira* (page 144).

Kale is readily available in the United States and like most leafy greens is thought to taste best after it has been hit by the first frost. Look for leaves that are unblemished and deep green. Many different vegetables can be used as a substitute for kale, notably collard greens and broccoli rabe.

CRABS. See *Caranguejo, Siri*

CRAVO-DA-ÍNDIA

(*Eugenia caryophyllata,* synonym *Syzygium aromaticum*) CLOVE

Brazilian desserts take some of their savor from a flavoring of whole or powdered cloves. This spice, which is native to the Moluccas in Southeast Asia, is prepared from the unopened flower buds of a tropical evergreen. It is so popular as a seasoning in Brazil that writer Jorge Amado used it in the title of one of his works in reference to the heroine: *Gabriela, Cravo e Canela — Gabriela, Clove and Cinnamon.*

Cloves, both whole and powdered, are readily available. As with all spices, purchase small quantities and store them away from the light in tightly sealed containers. Grind them in a spice grinder as you need them.

DENDÊ (*Elaeis guineensis*) OIL PALM

This palm tree which yields nuts that are processed into palm oil is a native of Africa, as its Latin name tells us. In Bahia the oil that is produced from the nuts is called *dendê* and is one of the hallmarks of Afro-Bahian food.

There is much controversy about tropical oils. With their high saturated-fat content, they tend to increase blood cholesterol levels in some people. However, because so many people have become aware of the cholesterol debate without knowing the scope of the issue, it must also be noted that according to an article that appeared in the

February 1987 *FDA Consumer Magazine,* "All foods of plant origin are essentially cholesterol-free. . . . However, they do contain varying amounts of fat." Warnings about elevated cholesterol levels should not be taken lightly. The debate is only beginning, with new information becoming available almost daily. Today even specialists on the subject, and I am not one, agree that much more research still needs to be done. One area coming under scrutiny is what happens when certain foods are eaten in combination with other foods (for example, palm oil and chiles).

With regard to the palm oil that is called for in the recipes in this book, it is called by its Brazilian name, *dendê*. And it can be replaced in several ways: It can be reduced by using a mixture of palm oil and the cook's polyunsaturated oil of preference; or it can be replaced by using a mixture of a cup of any polyunsaturated oil in which three tablespoons of annatto seeds have been soaked for twelve hours (see page 52); or it can be replaced by a polyunsaturated oil. In this last case, however, the taste will be completely different and if authenticity is what you crave, it is best not to attempt the recipe. There is a fourth option. Simply use the palm oil in moderation. If you have no medical contraindications and don't make a daily habit of it, it shouldn't hurt you.

Ironically, while palm oil presents problems for Americans, it is lauded in Brazil as an excellent source of vitamin A. Some even go so far as to say that the healthy complexions of many Bahians is due to their high use of palm oil.

A final word on palm oil. Brazilian palm oil is lighter in taste and texture than its West African counterpart. As the West African product is more readily available in Latin American, West Indian, and African markets, you may have to venture far afield to a Brazilian shop or mail order from one of the sources in the appendix to get a true Brazilian taste.

ERVA-DOCE (*Pimpinella anisum*) ANISE
This aromatic herb turns up occasionally in Brazilian cooking where it is an obvious European import from the Mediterranean basin. It is used as a carminative (relieves flatulence) and is thought to soothe the stomach. It is infused and consumed as a tea, and turns up in several dessert recipes, and in an unusual appetizer where it appears as a dipping oil (see page 76).

FARINHA DE MANDIOCA. See *Aipim*

FEIJÃO BEANS

In Brazil the bean is king. They should be. Beans were an important part of the diets of many of the people who came together to make up the Brazilian people.

Early chronicles mention beans among the foods consumed in the region prior to European arrival. Beans were also a part of the diet of the Portuguese early on. Mentions of something known as beans appear in texts as early as the thirteenth century. It would seem that pre-European Africa was extremely fond of beans, particularly the northern and western parts of the continent. Chroniclers mention that the Wolof of Senegambia cultivated many types of beans and the Mandingo grew red, black, and white beans. The Ibo and Yoruba from what would become Nigeria and Benin were noted for their fondness for white beans and black-eyed peas (which are actually beans—not peas!). In Brazil these tastes would become so national in scope that in 1826 Carl Seidler would write in his account of his ten years in Brazil, "There is no meal without beans, as only beans kill hunger."

The black bean, or *feijão preto*, is the preferred national bean. However, cowpeas, black-eyed peas, red beans, white beans, pink beans, among others, turn up in heavy burlap sacks in markets throughout the country. On Brazilian tables, they appear in dishes ranging from the national dish, *Feijoada*, to regional specialties like Minas Gerais's *Tutu a Mineira* (page 144) and São Paulo's *Virado a Paulista*, which are two variations on the mashed bean and cassava meal theme.

There are two basic methods for cooking dried beans—the overnight soak and the quick soak.

METHOD I—OVERNIGHT SOAK

This is the method that is traditionally used in Brazil in preparing everything from *Acarajé* (see page 59) to *Feijoada* (see page 171).

Pick over the beans, removing any stones or damaged ones. For ½ pound of dried beans, soak in 3 to 4 cups of cold water overnight. The next day they will have plumped and be ready for preparation.

This is a rapid way to attain the same results.

Place ½ pound of dried beans in 3 to 4 cups of cold water in a medium-size saucepan and bring them to a boil. Boil for 2 minutes, then remove them from the heat and allow them to sit for 1 hour. They, too, will be plumped and ready to prepare.

Whichever method is chosen, the beans should be drained and rinsed before proceeding. Also remember this hint from my non-Brazilian mother. Beans should always be started by cooking in COLD water. If water must be added at a later stage, it should always be HOT or the beans will be tough.

When purchasing beans, it is always wiser to buy them dried, by the pound or packaged, not precooked in cans. Many of the recipes calling for beans will simply not work if you attempt to substitute canned beans for soaked dry ones. Always pick over the beans before putting them in to soak; while processing is infinitely better in the United States than in Brazil with regard to debris, you can still find stones and bits of pebbles that would make a very unappetizing mouthful, so look carefully.

FOLHA DE BANANA. See *Banana*

GENGIBRE (*Zingiber officinale*) GINGER
Ginger puts the zing in many Bahian dishes and desserts. In fact, I was surprised when I began my research just how many times this rhizome turned up. Early chroniclers tell of the Brazilian Indians' abuse of ginger to the point that it gave them digestive difficulties. Ginger appears in main dishes like *Ximxim de Galinha* (page 184), and, in the northeast, in a locally brewed fermented ginger beer that is known as *gengibirra*. Because the cork of the ginger beer is kept in place with a cord or string, it is also known locally as *champanha de cordão*.

Ginger rhizomes are available virtually everywhere. Select young ones that are not too wrinkled and neither soft nor fibrous. If fresh ginger cannot be obtained, powdered ginger may be substituted, but remember to adjust the seasoning, as ground gingers vary in pungency.

GERGELIM (*Sesamum indicum*) SESAME

Sesame is used in the preparation of Brazilian sweets where it is occasionally roasted and mixed in with peanuts. It is interesting to note that the Portuguese language got its word for sesame from one of India's many languages, *gengily*.

GINGER. See *Gengibre*

GOIABA (*Psidium guajava*) GUAVA

There are over one hundred varieties of this fruit that is native to the Americas, but not to Brazil. Brazil's guavas are thought to have originally come from Peru thanks to birds that ate them and then left the seeds in bird droppings. Anyhow, they thrived and today are used in dessert compotes, in sweets, in juices, and eaten raw.

Guavas are becoming increasingly more available. If you find them, look for fruit that is firm with no blemishes. If fresh guavas are unavailable, canned ones can be used in preparing desserts and compotes.

HABANERO PEPPER. See *Pimenta-do-Cheiro*

HEARTS OF PALM. See *Palmito*

HORTELÃ (*Mentha viridis*) MINT

Mint appears in infusions in Brazil and less frequently in condiments and desserts.

Most forms of mint are readily available fresh in the United States. In fact, the adventurous gardener may find that mint will grow quite well in a window box or a small herb garden. Fresh mint is to be preferred, but if you're in a pinch, dried mint leaves can be substituted, just decrease the quantity by half.

INHAME TRUE YAM

That's right, there's no Latin name. That's because there is so much confusion over what is and is not a true yam. Various members of the *Dioscoreaceae* family have the honor. One thing, though, is sure, the orange-skinned tuber that passes for a yam in the American south is not a true yam. True yams abound and the hairy tubers are found in Brazilian markets under a variety of names, like white or African yam (*Colocasia antiquorum*), also known simply as yam, Indian yam (*Dioscorea alata*), and red yam (*Alocasia indica*).

Yams are used in purees and in *pirões* and are deep fried as vegetables. They also appear in stews. In another guise, they are transformed into ritual food and are served in Candomblé *terreiros* around the country at the beginning of the ritual year at the annual yam feasts for Oxaguian, the young warrior *orixá*, in a ceremony called *pilão de Oxaguian*. The *orixá's* name is a contraction of *Oxala-gui-yan* or Oxala-who-eats-yam.

Many varieties of yams can be found in Latin American markets. Look for ones that are firm with no sign of mold or insects. Larger yams—and some can grow to weigh as much as a quarter of a ton—are sold in pieces. Look for pieces that are not spongy or soft.

JENIPAPO (*Genipa americana*) GENIPAP

This tropical fruit is one that I have found only in Brazil. There it is used in the north and northeast in a sweet called *jenipapada* which is prepared by cutting the fruit pulp up and mixing it with sugar, and in the preparation of a delicious local liqueur. It can also be eaten raw.

KALE. See *Couve*

LAGOSTA SPINY LOBSTER

Unlike its cousins from Maine or New England, *lagosta* has no pincer claws. It makes up for this by having some of the tastiest meat of any lobster. In the coastal areas of Brazil, *lagosta* is served in a variety of ways. However, the most popular is grilled.

Lagosta are occasionally found in specialty fish markets. If you can find them, prepare them according to any of the lobster recipes I've included. If not, you can substitute lobster tails or even Maine lobsters, but you will not have the delicate taste.

LARANJA (*Citrus aurantium*) ORANGE

There are several varieties of oranges available in Brazil. The majority of the country's citrus—limes, lemons, and oranges—were brought by the Portuguese in the first half of the sixteenth century, but there are some oranges native to the country. Interestingly, the North American citrus industry was originally based on orange trees shipped from Bahia, Brazil.

In Brazil oranges are used in salads and in juices and in the preparation of drinks.

Readily available year-round throughout the United States, oranges need no explanation. Be sure to look for firm, ripe, juicy ones with no soft spots.

LEITE DE COCO. See *Coco*

LIMÃO (Citrus limon) LEMON
Brazilian lemons are green skinned and more tart in taste than their North American cousins. They are used in a variety of ways in Brazil similar to their uses in the Caribbean. No fish is cooked without first being marinated in lemon juice and the fruit itself is an ingredient in some dishes. It turns up in lemonades and in drinks like batidas. Several sauces use it instead of vinegar as their base. Most importantly for many people, bits of the fruit turn up in the bottom of caipirinha glasses around the country.

Because of the sharp taste of Brazilian lemons, I have suggested throughout the book that they be replaced in recipes by fresh limes.

Limes are readily available year-round. Select firm, juicy ones that have no blemishes or soft spots.

LINGÜIÇA PORTUGUESE SAUSAGE
This sausage, like its close cousin chouriço (see page 37), is prepared from pork, salt, onion, garlic, bay leaf, and black pepper according to various home recipes throughout the country.

Lingüiça is available in Portuguese markets around the country. Check also with mail-order sources. If you can't locate it, chorizo is an acceptable substitute.

LOBSTER. See *Lagosta*

MALAGUETA PEPPER. See *Pimenta Malagueta*

MANDIOCA. See *Aipim*

MANGA (*Mangifera indica*) MANGO

There are numerous varieties of mango available in Brazil. There are over 326 varieties registered in India and in Southeast Asia where the fruit is believed to have originated. It is thought that mangoes first made their way to Brazil in the second half of the eighteenth century, though some scholars place their arrival as early as the fifteenth. Whenever they arrived, they thrived and today, according to one scholar, over 500 different varieties of mango have been recorded in Brazil. They are used in desserts, in compotes, in candies, and in drinks, as well as being savored raw by everyone from schoolchildren to adults.

Whatever variety of mango you find, and they are becoming increasingly available in the United States, look for fruit that is firm, but yields slightly to the touch. A sniff will tell you if they're aromatic. For those who do not like the fibrousness of some mangoes, think of trying a green one. They're astringently tart and quite refreshing.

MANIOC. See *Aipim*

MARACUJÁ (*Passiflora edulis*) PASSION FRUIT

Named because the stamen and pistil of the flowers of the plant are thought by some to resemble the elements of Christ's passion, and not for the passion it inspires in its fans, passion fruit is one of the most popular Brazilian fruits. The small black seeds encased in tart translucent flesh provide flavoring for some of the country's most popular drinks and desserts.

Thanks to tropical fruit specialists in Florida and in California, passion fruit are becoming more available. If you can find them, the color of the skin and the degree of wrinkle make little difference as the taste is all in the fruit pulp encased in the yellow or purple shell. If passion fruit is not obtainable, it can be replaced by more readily available passion fruit pulp or passion fruit juice, which can be found frozen in shops in Latin American and Caribbean neighborhoods.

MILHO (*Zea mays*) CORN

Corn is used many ways in the Brazilian diet. Fresh corn is roasted or grilled or cooked with water and salt in various soups. Corn also appears in the form of cornmeal, called *fubá*, and which is used in the preparation of sweets, crackers, and cookies and in several starchy mashes called *angu* or *pirão*. Popcorn, called by its Tupi-Guarani name *pipoca*, is found frequently and is even used ritually in the Candomblé *terreiros* of Bahia (see page 9). White hominy corn is used in the preparation of dishes like *Canjica* (see page 224) and corn oil also appears in some dishes.

MINT. See *Hortelã*

MIRLTON SQUASH. See *Xuxu*

MORTEIRO E PILÃO MORTAR AND PESTLE

No Brazilian kitchen is complete without at least one mortar in which the cook prepares sauces and grinds herbs and seasonings. In rural households a large mortar may be kept for such tasks as grinding grains.

While a food processor can replace much of the grinding work, it cannot always give the same consistency, particularly when working with nuts or herbs and spices. Try both methods and see which you prefer.

In Brazil pestles frequently do double duty as pounders and implements to mix the sugar and lime juice in caipirinhas.

NAJE

This low-sided, flat-bottom clay cooking vessel is the pot of choice for much Bahian cooking. It is perfect for this because it sits comfortably on the burners of the traditional wood-burning stoves still used in many homes and restaurants and it evenly distributes the heat.

Naje are not available in the United States, but if you're going to Brazil, or know someone who is, you might wish to obtain one and experiment. Indeed, they allow dishes like *moquecas* and *ensopados* to cook perfectly. If not, any heavy cooking pot can and will replace them with little difference.

ORANGE. See *Laranja*

PALMITO (*Palmae family*) HEARTS OF PALM

This is the white, tender inner portion of several palm species. It is served fresh or pickled and is a delicacy in many Brazilian households and restaurants, though not nearly as expensive there as it is in the United States. In Florida, where it is known as swamp cabbage, *palmito* is also common. In Brazil *palmito* is eaten raw as an accompaniment to *churrasco* or cooked in stews. In the Amazon region, it is a favorite dish of the Brazilian Indians and is even used as a cure for beriberi.

If you are fortunate enough to live in Florida near lots of it or in an area where fresh *palmito* appears from time to time, it is easily prepared by removing the coarse outer husk and boiling the heart in water and lemon juice to cover until it is fork tender. If not, you can purchase canned hearts of palm at supermarkets and specialty shops throughout the country.

PALM OIL. See *Dendê*

PASSION FRUIT. See *Maracujá*

PEANUTS. See *Amendoim*

PIMENTA MALAGUETA (*Capsicum annuum*) MALAGUETA PEPPER

This is to much of Brazilian cooking what salt and black pepper are to much of European cooking, the primary seasoning. It appears preserved in small bottles or fresh and transformed into various sauces on tables throughout the country. First and foremost, remember that even though they're called malagueta peppers both in English and in Portuguese, these are in fact chiles and as such should be handled with care to avoid chile burns (see note on page 49). These chiles are not to be confused with melegueta peppers which are also called grains of paradise, a cousin of black pepper that was used in West Africa prior to the European arrival. Although most malagueta peppers are similar to bird peppers, some bottles of malagueta peppers also include tabasco chiles which are from the *Capsicum frutescens* species.

Malagueta peppers are not found fresh in the United States. The tabasco chiles can be, particularly in the south and southwest, and are an acceptable substitute. Preserved malagueta peppers can be obtained from Brazilian stores and from the mail-order sources in the appendix.

NOTE: Chiles, both fresh and dry, contain highly volatile oils that can irritate and even burn skin and eyes. Those unaccustomed to working with chiles, and even a few of those who are, should therefore take care to protect their hands when working with them. Some prefer to use rubber gloves, others opt to coat their skin with oil before working with them. If, despite precautions, you feel a slight tingling, soak your hands in milk. If you should get chile oil in your eyes, flush them immediately with cold water.

PIMENTA-DO-CHEIRO (*Capsicum chinense*) HABANERO CHILE

The habanero chile is reputed to be the world's hottest. They have been tested at a range between 200,000 and 300,000 Scoville units and register a whopping 10, the highest possible, on the heat scale. The Amazon Basin supports the world's largest number of habanero varieties. These chiles appear in a variety of ways in Brazilian cooking, particularly that of the northeastern region. They are chopped and put into homemade sauces and pickled and show up on the table as condiments.

Habanero chiles can be easily found if you live near a West Indian neighborhood. There they are called by their Jamaican name, Scotch bonnet, and are available at greengrocers' shops. If you find and are using them, remember to handle with care to avoid chile burns (see note on how to handle peppers in above entry). Also remember these chiles are HOT! If you cannot find habanero-type chiles, you can replace them with any hot chile; however, as the habanero chile adds not only heat but flavor to dishes, the result will be something slightly different than the true taste of Brazil. You can also order preserved *pimenta-do-cheiro* from the mail-order sources in the appendix.

PIMENTA-DO-REINO (*Piper nigrum*) BLACK PEPPER

For Brazilians, this is called "pepper from the kingdom," for during colonial times, all black pepper was imported to Portugal from the

Spice Islands and thence to Brazil. Today Brazil is an exporter of black peppercorns which are quite pungent, if not as sought after as the famed Indian Tellicherry pepper.

Whenever you use black or white pepper, grind your own. A pepper mill is an inexpensive addition to any kitchen and the difference in pungency between home ground black pepper and the drab tinned version that is occasionally adulterated with other less expensive items is incredible. Black peppercorns are readily available at supermarkets and at gourmet food shops.

PINEAPPLE. See *Abacaxi*

PIPOCA. See *Milho*

PIRARUCÚ (*Arapaima gigas*)

This large Amazon fish is one of the staples of the diet of the Amazon region. Its flesh turns up grilled in thick fish steaks or on skewers, marinated and in baked local dishes like *pirarucú no horno* and dried like *charque* (see page 36) and called *bacalhau da Amazonia*.

Pirarucú cannot be found in the United States and it has been replaced in recipes by other firm white-fleshed fish.

PUMPKIN. See *Abóbora*

QUIABO (*Hibiscus esculentus*) OKRA

Although it is perhaps one of the least-liked vegetables in the Western world, okra is one of Africa's gifts to Brazilian cooking where it is much appreciated. Okra is used in the cooking of Bahia where it is stewed, put in salads, and simply boiled. It also turns up in African-inspired dishes like *Carurú* (page 200) and *Quiabada* (page 175). Unlike most North Americans, Brazilians do not try to work against okra's natural tendency to be slippery. Instead, they use the slipperiness to enhance the dishes in which it is an ingredient.

Okra is readily available almost year-round in markets in African-American and Caribbean neighborhoods and throughout the South. When selecting fresh okra, look for small pods that are about the size of a little finger. They should have no blemishes and not be large or woody. Okra is also available canned or frozen. If you are reduced to using one of these, frozen is preferable. There are two points to remember when cooking okra: 1) the longer you cook it, the slimier it gets; 2) the more you cut okra, the slimier it gets.

RICE. See *Arroz*

SARDINHA (*Sardina pilchardus*) SARDINES

This ocean fish is the small fry of the herring family. It can be eaten fresh or processed. This is undoubtedly one taste that the Brazilians have inherited from their Portuguese forebearers because Portugal is still known as one of the finest producers of canned sardines in the world. In Brazil the sardines are used fresh, grilled, or baked. They are even found flattened out in local street markets in Rio to facilitate these uses. Canned ones appear in dishes such as *Cuscuz Brasileiro* which appears on page 81.

Canned sardines are available virtually everywhere. You can find them canned in olive oil or in a tomatoey sauce. For the recipes that call for canned sardines in this book, use those canned in olive oil. Fresh sardines are more difficult to come by. When you find them, select the freshest-looking ones of uniform size.

SAUSAGE. See *Chouriço, Lingüiça*

SESAME. See *Gergelim*

SHRIMP. See *Camarão, Camarão Seco*

SIRI (*Portunidae* species) CRAB

These are the more typical seafaring cousins of the *caranguejos* (see page 35). They are frequently found on menus in the coastal regions of the country and are served stuffed or simply boiled and accompanied by a *pimenta malagueta* sauce.

When *siri* are called for, fresh crabs or fresh lump crabmeat can be used. Both are readily available in many parts of the country. If fresh lump crabmeat cannot be found, frozen crabmeat may be substituted.

TAPIOCA

This is cassava meal that has been roasted and granulated. In Brazil it is much loved and much used. It is mixed with grated coconut and transformed into desserts or simply mixed with water and served as a porridge. It is also served as a starchy mash to accompany main dishes.

Tapioca is readily available. Prepare it according to package directions.

TUCUPI

This condiment, which is indispensable to several dishes from the Amazon region, is prepared from the liquid that has been expressed from the cassava in the preparation of cassava meal. This liquid is boiled with garlic, chicory, malagueta pepper, and other ingredients. The liquid condiment is a main ingredient in the preparation of tucupi duck and *tucupi tacaca*, both Amazonian specialties.

Tucupi is virtually impossible to find outside of Brazil. For that reason, it is simply listed here and no dishes will call for it. If you are in Brazil, however, it is a condiment to bring back that will undoubtedly astound your friends.

URUCU (*Bixa orellana*) ANNATTO, ACHIOTE

These berries were originally gathered by the native Brazilians for their red juice which they use to decorate their bodies. The juice from the berries today adds color to cheeses and to rice. However, with the coming of the Africans to Brazilian shores, the berries found yet another use. When they are cooked with oil, they give it a reddish-orange color similar to that of palm oil. This *oleo de urucum* is used in the cooking of the Brazilian state of Espírito Santo in preference to *dendê*. To prepare it, place 3 tablespoons of annatto seed in a cup of oil and either steep for 12 hours or heat over a medium-low flame for 5 minutes until the oil is reddish orange. It will keep for a week in the refrigerator.

Annatto berries can be found in gourmet and herb and spice

shops or in Hispanic markets. They should be purchased in small quantities when they are brick red, as they lose their coloring properties and their faint taste once they turn brown.

VINHO WINE

Brazil is rapidly joining Argentina and Chile as one of the top wine producers of South America. The major wine-growing region is on the southern tip of the country, a region with a strong Italian influence. The style of the wines, then, is Italian as are the grapes, with the barbera producing fruity reds and the trebbiano, moscato, and malvasia most important in the production of the whites. While quality is improving annually, there are as yet no truly great Brazilian wines.

In addition to the red, white, and rosé wines produced from the *Vitis vinifira* grape, Brazil also produces many locally made and homemade wines from its bounty of fruit, notably the orange, mango, cashew, and pineapple wines of the northeast.

Brazilian wines are occasionally found in North American liquor stores. The reds are a good foil for the spicy tastes of Bahian food, while the whites pair off nicely with the seafood dishes.

WATERCRESS. See *Agrião*

XÍCARA CUP

No Brazilian kitchen can function without a teacup and a coffee cup, for these are the measures that appear most often in many of the country's traditional recipes.

XUXU (*Sechium edule*) CHAYOTE, MIRLITON SQUASH

This light pastel green squash is used in several Brazilian dishes. Its faint flavor allows it to take on the flavors of the ingredients which accompany it and makes it a natural for dishes where other, stronger flavors predominate.

The peel and seeds of the young chayote are edible. However, once the vegetable has matured, they should be discarded. Chayote are becoming readily available in supermarkets around the country.

Firm ones with no blemishes should be selected. If you cannot find chayote, you can substitute yellow summer squash or zucchini in most cases, but the taste will be stronger.

YAM. See *Inhame*

ZURRAPA

Just because it begins with a Z and it's a good place to end. This is a Brazilian term for any alcoholic drink or wine of poor quality.

SALGADINHOS

Appetizers

IN BRAZIL appetizers are an important part of the meal. They are consumed along with rum drinks or sodas while sharing news with friends and winding down to enjoy the meal. This can happen in restaurants or in homes. Appetizers are usually tasty small fried nibbles or occasionally such things as popcorn or even small pieces of toast with a variety of spreads. They are called *salgadinhos*, meaning "small salted things" or *tira gosto*, "taste pullers" and they are designed to whet the appetite for the meal to come. Many restaurants are known for the variety of *salgadinhos* they serve.

Bahian writer Jorge Amado tells the story of one noted maker of appetizer snacks in his novel *Gabriela, Cravo e Canela* (*Gabriela, Clove and Cinnamon*). In the novel, Gabriela, an excellent cook of small appetizers, wins the heart of not only the owner of the cafe but all of his patrons and goes from being a refugee from the droughts of the Sertão to being a respectable woman. The cafe owner even marries her. However, once married all is not well. Curious about the rest? Read the book, it's super. Or if you're lazy, catch the film which stars Brazilian bombshell Sonia Braga and none less than Marcello Mastroianni.

Dona Floripedes dos Guimaraes, another of the novelist Amado's literary cooks, is not only excellent at the stove, she also runs a cooking school called the the School of Savor and Art. Like

Gabriela, in her hands food is transformed into art. Amado, who is known in Bahia and throughout Brazil as a gourmet, includes several recipes in his novels and writes about food with a passion that many others apply only to matters carnal.

Gabriela and Dona Flor, though, are only products of the imagination. Throughout Brazil there are thousands like them who prepare small appetizers. Some work in cafes where no patron can sit down for a beer or a caipirinha without being given a plate of tidbits. Others work in their own kitchens or in the kitchens of others serving only family and friends. Still others have made a business from their abilities and peddle their appetizing snacks from trays at street corners in the large cities. In Bahia they can be found, decked out in traditional Bahian finery, on street corners and also along the beaches that lead out from the city with names like Jardim de Alá, Itapuã, and Pituba. Their trays and braziers have grown into small thatched huts where they prepare snacks for those who come to spend a day at the beach, and the menu has expanded a bit. Some have moved beyond the tray and the beach to become proprietors of their own restaurants like Mãe Analia Moreira Campos whose restaurant, Iemanja, pays homage to the Yoruba goddess of saltwater, or Maria de San Pedro, whose restaurant in the Mercado Modelo is where many tourists learn all they will ever know about Bahian cooking. One of the appetizers that is usually bubbling in the caldrons of these women who cook is *acarajé*, the spicy black-eyed pea fritters that are northeastern Brazil's most popular appetizer.

Acarajé

Black-eyed Pea Fritters

MAKES 4 TO 6 SERVINGS

The *Baianas de tabuleiro*, or Bahian ladies with trays, are frequently devotees of the Afro-Brazilian religion Candomblé, for many of the traditional recipes of Bahia come directly from the kitchens of the *terreiros* or Candomblé houses. The Yoruba gods, or *orixá*, of West Africa are gourmet gods and demand that their ritual meals are prepared exactingly. The *Iya Basse*, or head cook, of the *terreiros* is a martinet and puts her apprentices through a rigorous training that would make even Escoffier's eyes pop. In the *terreiro* of Casa Branca do Engenho Velho in Bahia, ritual demands that all of the dishes be prepared by hand over a wood-burning stove. No food processors, no mixers, and no gas stoves are used when the ritual meals are prepared to serve the hundreds that can turn up to eat at a ceremony.

Acarajé are the preferred dish of Yansã (or Oya as she is known in West Africa). This *orixá* is the goddess of the Niger River in Nigeria. However, in the New World she rules over tempests and winds. Her day is Wednesday and on the first Wednesday of every month her devotees in Brazil and around the world prepare her ritual food, *acarajé*. Her food, with secular variations, has gone from the *terreiro* to the street corner to become one of the most popular in Brazil. My friend in Bahia, Carmen, and my friend and daughter of Yansã in New York, Erminha, showed me this way with *acarajé*.

> **1 pound dried black-eyed peas, soaked (see page 41), drained, and rinsed**
>
> **½ cup water**
>
> **1 large onion, minced**
>
> **Salt and freshly ground black pepper to taste**
>
> **Dendê (see page 39) for deep frying or a mixture of ¼ dendê and ¾ vegetable oil**

Peel the outer skins off the soaked peas by rubbing them between your hands. Puree the peas in a blender or food processor, adding the water gradually until you have a thick paste. Fold in the onions and season. Heat 4 to 5 inches of oil in a deep cast-iron or other heavy pot to 350° to 375°F over medium-high heat. Drop in the bean paste a spoonful at a time. Do not place too many in the oil at once as they will lower the temperature and make frying difficult. When browned on one side, about 2 minutes, turn to brown on the other. When both sides are browned, remove the fritters with a slotted spoon and drain on paper towels. Serve plain or split as a sandwich with *Molho Acarajé* (recipe follows) or *Vatapá* (page 160).

Molho Acarajé

Acarajé Sauce

MAKES ABOUT 1 CUP

3 or 4 preserved malagueta peppers or to taste (see page 88)

½ cup dried smoked shrimp, minced (see page 35)

1 small onion, chopped

3 sprigs fresh coriander (cilantro), minced

½ teaspoon ground ginger

2 tablespoons dendê (see page 39)

Puree all of the ingredients together, except the *dendê*, in a blender or food processor until they form a paste. Heat the oil in a small, heavy saucepan over medium heat, then add the mixture and cook, stirring to combine, for 5 to 7 minutes. Cool and serve on split *acarajé*.

Pipoca

Popcorn

$\diamond$

Popcorn is a dish that is found on Brazilian tables as a predinner snack. As reported by noted Brazilian anthropologist and culinary historian Gilberto Freye, its name in Brazilian Portuguese comes from the word for cracked skin in Tupi-Guarani, a language spoken by the Amazonian Indians. In Bahia August is the month for popcorn, for it is the month of Omolu, the Candomblé *orixá* of smallpox and disease who is sometimes called the doctor of the poor. During the month, devotees of the Candomblé religion head out into the street dressed in their frothy white lace garments carrying wooden trays filled with popcorn and covered with pristine lace cloths. Those in the know in Bahia will always try to get a handful, as it is thought to protect them from disease. In this era of microwave popcorn, it's sometimes a treat to make it the old-fashioned way in which it is prepared in Brazil, with a heavy, lidded pot, some oil, and the popcorn.

> **4 to 6 tablespoons vegetable oil, or enough to coat the bottom of the pot**
>
> **⅓ cup popcorn kernels**
>
> **Salt to taste**

Coat the bottom of a heavy saucepan with the oil and heat it until one kernel of popcorn will pop when placed in it. Pour in the rest of the popcorn, cover the pot, and cook it over high heat, shaking it constantly, until the popping sounds stop. Remove from heat, season with salt, and serve hot.

Ovos de Codorniz

Quail Eggs

This is an appetizer that is commonly found on the tables of some of the best restaurants in Brazil. It consists of the old relish plate that used to be a familiar standby in family restaurants throughout the United States with the addition of small hard-boiled quail eggs.

8 quail eggs (see note below)

4 celery hearts, quartered

4 large carrots, thinly sliced into spears

6 scallions, trimmed

12 large black calamata olives

Place the quail eggs in a medium-size saucepan and cover with cold water. Bring to a boil and continue to boil for two minutes. Remove from the water and cool. Meanwhile, keep the prepared vegetables in the refrigerator in a glass of water with ice cubes. When ready to serve, arrange all of the ingredients on a small platter and place in the middle of the table.

NOTE: Raw quail eggs are available at gourmet food stores and, occasionally, at neighborhood markets.

Salsichas Fritas

Fried Sausage

MAKES 4 SERVINGS

One of my favorite Brazilian restaurants in New York City is called Via Brasil. I was first taken there by a friend who worked for the Brazilian Tourist Office and subsequently have taken numerous friends and family members. They have a selection of Brazilian appetizers and make wonderful caipirinhas and the best batidas in New York. The appetizer that I find goes best with my *Caipirinha de Maracujá* (see page 245) is this one which is simple to make at home.

> ½ pound Portuguese sausage, like lingüiça or
> chouriço (see note below), cut into
> ½-inch rounds
>
> 20 large black calamata olives

Fry the sausage rounds in a heavy iron skillet over medium-high heat until they are browned on both sides, about 5 minutes. Drain on paper towels and place on a serving platter with the olives. Serve.

NOTE: If Portuguese sausage cannot be found, select a mild Spanish chorizo.

Azeitonas Temperadas

Seasoned Olives

MAKES 8 TO 10 SERVINGS

This is a case of Brazilian cooks never leaving well enough alone and thereby coming up with something even better. Here regular black olives are used to create a spicy olive dish that is wonderful. You can use plain canned olives, but the better the olives are to start, the better they are at the end.

1 pound black olives

1 tablespoon dried oregano

2 teaspoons preserved malagueta peppers or to taste (see page 88)

2 tablespoons extra virgin olive oil

Prick each olive several times with the point of a knife. Place the olives and remaining ingredients in a bowl and mix well. Cover with plastic wrap and refrigerate for at least two hours for the flavors to mix. Serve chilled. They will keep in the refrigerator for about two weeks.

Azeitonas Recheadas com Filés de Enchovas

Anchovy-stuffed Olives

———— ◆ ————

I can only believe that this appetizer is a part of Brazil's Iberian heritage, for I first came into contact with anchovy-stuffed olives in Spain. However, they are delicious and are perfect with drinks and nuts or on a Brazilian relish dish. When you prepare them yourself, you can use large olives and you truly get the combination of the briny tang of the olive with the salty taste of the anchovy. Get the best of both that you can find. It's a time-consuming recipe, but it's worth it.

½ **pound pitted large green olives**

**One 2-ounce can flat anchovy fillets, drained
and cut into pieces**

Stuff each olive with a piece of anchovy. If they are not going to be served immediately, keep them in the refrigerator in a glass jar with the olive brine, up to several days.

Cebolinhas no Vinagre

Shallots in Vinegar

MAKES 4 TO 6 SERVINGS

These pickled onions turn up on the ever-present relish trays at homey Brazilian restaurants and are always a pleasant and tasty surprise. As the small bitey red onions that are found in markets in Cachoeira and other spots in Brazil are not readily available in the United States, I have substituted shallots which have a similar tang.

  1 pound shallots, peeled

  4 cups water

  2 cups red wine vinegar

  Salt to taste

  6 black peppercorns

  3 cloves garlic, peeled

  ½ lemon, thinly sliced

  2 bay leaves

Place the shallots in a large heavy nonreactive saucepan with the remaining ingredients. Bring the liquid to a boil, then remove the shallots from the heat and allow them to cool. Place them in sterilized jars and chill. Serve along with celery, carrot sticks, and olives on a Brazilian-type relish dish. They will keep in the refrigerator for about two weeks.

Enchovas

Spicy Brazilian Anchovies

MAKES 4 TO 6 SERVINGS

Hot spicy anchovies are the basis for this spread which can be adjusted to fit the amount of chile (heat) you enjoy.

One 2-ounce can flat anchovy fillets

4 preserved malagueta peppers minced, or to taste (see page 88)

1 small onion, minced

1 clove garlic, minced

1 tablespoon extra virgin olive oil

Place all of the ingredients in a blender or food processor and puree until you have a fine paste. Spoon the paste into a bowl, cover it with plastic wrap, and refrigerate for 24 hours to allow the tastes to mix. Serve at room temperature with toast or crackers. The paste will keep in the refrigerator for about one week.

Castanha-do-Pará

Brazil Nuts

With all of the nibbling and munching that goes on before a Brazilian lunch or dinner, it is only fitting that there should be nuts served as well. The nuts that most come to mind when the country's name is mentioned are the rough, dark-brown-shelled ones that are called Brazil nuts in the English-speaking world. These indeed are served to accompany drinks. They are readily available shelled and un-shelled. To get a truly Brazilian taste, try toasting them for a few minutes in the broiler and then dusting them lightly with salt.

1 pound shelled Brazil nut meats

2 tablespoons pure olive oil

Salt to taste

Preheat the broiler. Arrange the nut meats on a cookie sheet and drizzle the olive oil over them. Place them under the broiler for 2 to 3 minutes, or until they are heated through. Remove the nuts, pat them dry with paper towels, and place them in a paper bag with the salt. Shake the nuts to coat them with the salt and serve warm with cocktails.

Aipim Frita

Fried Sweet Cassava

MAKES 6 TO 8 SERVINGS

This is a dish that is found not only in Brazil but throughout the Hispanic Caribbean. The sweet, slightly bland taste of the sweet cassava lends itself well to frying. A little cassava meal gives a bit of extra crunch.

1 pound sweet cassava, cut into french fry-like pieces (see page 29)

¼ cup cassava meal (see page 31)

Vegetable oil for frying

In a large, heavy iron pot, heat 4 to 5 inches of oil to 350° to 375°F over medium-high heat. Wash the sweet cassava pieces and pat them dry with paper towels. Place them a few at a time into a bag in which you have placed the cassava meal and shake to coat. Remove from the meal and fry a few at a time until lightly browned, about 3 to 5 minutes. Remove them from the oil with a slotted spoon and drain on paper towels. Serve hot.

Banana de Terra Frita

Fried Plantain

MAKES 4 SERVINGS

This is a dish that can be served many ways. When prepared from green plantains, as in the recipe below, the result is fried plantain chips which are good as an appetizer. When prepared with ripe plantains, the dish is transformed into a Bahian specialty which is traditionally served as an accompaniment to fish dishes. When prepared with overripe plantains and sprinkled with sugar and ground cinnamon, the dish becomes a dessert.

4 large green plantains

½ cup vegetable oil

½ cup dendê (see page 39)

Salt to taste

Peel the plantains under running water and cut them into thin rounds. Mix the oils together in a heavy saucepan and heat them to 350°F to 375°F over medium-high heat. (If you are wary of *dendê,* you can use all vegetable oil. However, the taste will be different.) Drop the plantain slices in the oil a few at a time and fry until they are golden brown. Remove the slices, drain them on paper towels, and sprinkle with salt. Serve warm.

Coquetel de Camarão

Shrimp Cocktail

MAKES 4 SERVINGS

In the coastal regions of Brazil, shrimp abound and are used in many different ways, from soups to salads to main dishes. They are used fresh and smoked and dried. They also turn up in a variety of appetizer cocktails which are served in restaurants large and small and in homes. This version is the shrimp cocktail as prepared by my friend Nair.

⅓ cup plain yogurt

1 small onion, minced

1 teaspoon grated fresh horseradish

1 teaspoon minced preserved malagueta pepper (see page 88)

3 tablespoons tomato paste

Salt and freshly ground black pepper to taste

1 pound cooked jumbo shrimp (see page 34)

Lettuce leaves for garnish

Mix all the ingredients, except the shrimp and lettuce, together in a small bowl to make a cocktail sauce. When ready to serve, place the sauce in a small bowl in the middle of a platter, arrange the shrimp on lettuce leaves around the bowl, and serve cold.

Coquetel de Lagosta

Lobster cocktail

Where shrimp go, can lobster be far behind? This lobster salad appetizer can also be prepared with shrimp or with cooked crabmeat. The bite comes from the sauce, *Molho Rita,* which I learned from my Bahian friend, Rita.

> **2 cooked lobster tails**
>
> **1 small head Boston lettuce, separated into leaves**
>
> **1 large ripe tomato, peeled, seeded, and coarsely chopped**
>
> **1 small onion, minced**
>
> **2 tablespoons Molho Rita (see page 98) or to taste**
>
> **Salt and freshly ground black pepper to taste**
>
> **1 bunch fresh parsley for garnish**

Remove the lobster meat from the tail shells and cut it into slices crosswise to get ½-inch-thick rounds of lobster. Arrange the lettuce leaves on a platter or individual serving dishes. Place the lobster rounds on the lettuce and sprinkle with the tomato and onion. Then drizzle with the *molho rita.* Season and garnish with sprigs of parsley. Serve chilled.

Bolinho de Peixe

Fish Balls

MAKES 4 TO 6 SERVINGS

Tasty fried tidbits are a major part of the Brazilian way with appetizers. These fish balls from Bahia are an atypical example because they are prepared from fish that has already been fried, which makes them perfect for using up leftovers.

> 1 pound fried fish fillets (see page 192)
>
> 1 medium-size onion, minced
>
> ¼ cup pitted green olives, minced
>
> 1 teaspoon minced habanero-type chile or to taste (see page 49)
>
> Salt and freshly ground black pepper to taste
>
> 2 large eggs
>
> 2 tablespoons milk
>
> Vegetable oil for frying
>
> 2 tablespoons flour

Pick over the fish fillets to remove any stray bones, then shred the fish and place it in a large bowl. Add the onion, olives, chile, and seasonings to the fish and mix well. In a second bowl, beat the eggs, then add the milk, stirring to make sure they are well mixed. Add the egg mixture to the fish mixture, again stirring well to combine. Meanwhile, heat 4 inches of oil to 350° to 375°F over medium heat in a large heavy saucepan. Roll the fish mixture into balls and cover them with flour. Drop the fish mixture into the oil and fry until golden brown on both sides, 2 to 3 minutes. (Do not try to fry too many at once as you will lower the temperature of the oil and lengthen the cooking time.) Remove the balls with a slotted spoon, drain on paper towels, and serve hot with *Molho Rita* (see page 98) or *Molho de Pimenta e Limão* (page 93).

Pitú

Crayfish Brazilian Style

MAKES 4 SERVINGS

Not only is *pitú* the name of my favorite cachaça (Brazilian sugarcane brandy), it is also the name for the saltwater crayfish that frequently appear on menus in the northeast. The hardest thing with crayfish is deciding how many to suggest serving per person. They are delicious and highly habit-forming. What begins to be a crayfish appetizer frequently ends up as a crayfish lunch or dinner. Be forewarned and have enough. For appetizer portions, I'm suggesting five per person.

> **20 fresh crayfish**
>
> **2 quarts water**
>
> **1 small onion, thinly sliced**
>
> **1 medium-size ripe tomato, peeled, seeded, and coarsely chopped**
>
> **4 limes, cut into wedges for garnish**

Wash the crayfish with saltwater or, better yet, with sea water. Bring the water to a boil in a heavy saucepan along with the onion, tomato, and a bit of the lime zest. Drop in the crayfish and cook them until they turn red. Remove, drain, and serve garnished with lime wedges along with your favorite hot sauce. This is a dish that is best when eaten with the fingers. Break off the heads and suck out all of the meat you can get. Yum!

Crostini

Cheese Toasts

MAKES 4 SERVINGS

These small bread bits are topped with a mixture of Parmesan and Gruyère cheese and toasted in the broiler until the cheese melts. For those who like things less spicy, omit the minced malagueta pepper.

> **4 tablespoons (½ stick) butter, at room temperature**
>
> **2 tablespoons freshly grated Parmesan cheese**
>
> **2 tablespoons freshly grated Gruyère or Swiss cheese**
>
> **½ teaspoon minced preserved malagueta pepper or to taste (see page 88)**
>
> **8 slices bread, crusts removed and cut into quarters**
>
> **Salt and freshly grated white pepper to taste**

Preheat the broiler. Mix the butter and cheeses together. Add the malagueta pepper and mix well. Spread the mixture on top of each quarter of bread, then season. Arrange the bread pieces on an ungreased cookie sheet and place under the broiler. Cook for 2 minutes, or until the cheese becomes golden brown. (Watch carefully because the cheese goes from golden to black in what seems like an instant!) Serve warm with cocktails.

Erva-Doce

Anise Oil

MAKES ABOUT ¾ CUP

This licorice-flavored olive oil makes an interesting dipping sauce for Italian bread for this appetizer from the southern part of Brazil.

2 teaspoons aniseed

6 tablespoons extra virgin olive oil

2 tablespoons fresh lemon juice

2 tablespoons water

Salt and freshly ground white pepper to taste

Mix all of the ingredients together in a small ceramic (nonreactive) bowl. It will keep in the refrigerator for up to one week.

Bolinhos de Queijo

Cheese Balls

MAKES 4 TO 6 SERVINGS

Salgadinhos are small, usually savory, fried appetizers that are a large part of Brazil's before-dinner rituals. They are frequently balls of fish, cheese, or vegetables which are served with a variety of spicy sauces. These cheese balls would be prepared from the wonderful white cheese that comes from Minas Gerais in Brazil. Here, I have substituted a mixture of mozzarella and Parmesan.

> ½ **pound Parmesan cheese, freshly grated**
>
> ½ **pound mozzarella cheese, freshly grated**
>
> **3 large egg whites**
>
> **2 heaping tablespoons flour**
>
> **Vegetable oil for frying**

Mix the cheeses together in a large glass or ceramic bowl. Beat the egg whites into stiff peaks in another large bowl, add them to the cheese, and fold in well. Form the mixture into balls and roll them in the flour. Meanwhile, heat 4 to 5 inches of oil in a large heavy saucepan to 350° to 375°F over medium-high heat. Drop in the cheese balls a few at a time and fry them until they are golden brown. Remove them with a slotted spoon and drain them on paper towels. Serve hot with cocktails.

Bolinhos de Bacalhau

Codfish Balls

MAKES 4 SERVINGS

These codfish balls are perhaps the most typical of all *salgadinhos*. They appear on Brazilian tables in myriad variations. Inventive cooks incorporate hot chiles, minced onion, herbs, spices, and other ingredients into the basic salt codfish mixture. This recipe calls for mashed potatoes.

½ pound dried codfish, reconstituted (see page 31) and flaked

1 cup mashed potatoes

4 large eggs, separated

1 small onion, minced

1 tablespoon minced fresh parsley

Salt and freshly ground black pepper to taste

Vegetable oil for frying

Mix the flaked codfish, mashed potatoes, egg yolks, onion, parsley, and seasonings together in a large bowl. Stir the mixture together well. Beat the egg whites into stiff peaks in a large bowl, then fold them into the codfish mixture. Roll the mixture into small balls. Heat 4 to 5 inches of oil in a large, heavy saucepan to 350° to 375°F over medium-high heat and drop the balls into the oil a few at a time. Fry them until they are golden brown, 3 to 5 minutes. Remove them with a slotted spoon, drain on paper towels, and serve warm.

DOIS PARA SANDWICHES
Two Sandwich Spreads

In Brazil another appetizer is various spreads that can be used on toast points or breadsticks. Sometimes they are no more than savory garlic butters. Other times they are complicated mixtures of shrimp and mayonnaise or onions and Parmesan cheese. Whatever the mixture, they are an interesting addition to a relish plate and a good way for inventive cooks to have fun. Here are two examples.

Camarão e Maionese

Shrimp and Mayonnaise

MAKES 4 SERVINGS

This spread is popular in Rio where the shrimp are readily available.

16 cooked large shrimp, diced (see page 34)

¼ cup mayonnaise

16 pimiento-stuffed green olives, minced

Place all of the ingredients together in a small bowl. Mix well and chill for 1 hour. When ready, serve the spread in a ramekin with toast points on the side.

Castanhas do Caju e Queijo

Cashews and Cheese

MAKES 4 SERVINGS

In this variation the mixture is spread on bread which is then toasted in a hot oven.

½ cup freshly grated Gruyère

½ cup freshly grated Parmesan

1 teaspoon sweet paprika

2 tablespoons minced onion

8 slices white bread

3 tablespoons chopped cashew nuts

Preheat the broiler. Mix the cheeses, paprika, and onion together in a small bowl, then spread on the bread. Place the bread slices on an ungreased cookie sheet and place them under the broiler until the cheese melts and is golden brown on top (watch carefully—this happens quickly). Remove the sandwiches from the oven, cut them into quarters, and sprinkle the cashew nuts over each quarter. Serve hot.

Abará

Bahian Steamed Bean Cakes

MAKES 6 SERVINGS

This is a classic Bahian appetizer similar in taste to *acarajé* (see page 59). In this case, though, the bean mixture is boiled in a banana leaf and not fried in *dendê*.

1 pound dried black-eyed peas, soaked (see page 41), drained, and rinsed

1 tablespoon dendê (see page 39)

¼ pound dried smoked shrimp (see page 35)

½ cup grated onion

3 banana leaves (see page 33)

2 quarts water

Salt and preserved malagueta pepper to taste

Peel the skins from the soaked beans by rubbing them between your hands. Place the beans in a blender or food processor and pulse until you have a smooth paste. Add the *dendê*, shrimp, onion, salt and malagueta pepper to the bean mixture, stirring well to combine.

Prepare the banana leaves according to the directions on page 33. Then place a few tablespoons of the bean mixture into a piece of banana leaf and wrap it tightly. Boil the water in a large saucepan or stockpot. When the water is boiling, add the stuffed leaves and allow them to cook. You'll know when they're done because they will rise to the top. Remove them to a plate with a slotted spoon.

The *abará* are served in their leaves. Unwrap and eat them at the table or as snacks.

Cuscuz Brasileiro

Brazilian Couscous

MAKES 8 SERVINGS

This dish owes its name to the Moorish occupation of Portugal. However, this couscous bears only a faint resemblance to its North

African homonym. There are many different types of couscous in Brazil. They range from savory, like this one, to sweet dessert ones like the *cuscuz amarela* and the *cuscuz branca* from the northeast which are prepared with cornmeal or tapioca and are closer in style to the sweet couscouses of North Africa. This one, which also appears on menus as *cuscuz paulista,* is a molded casserole of sardines, shrimp, onions, cornmeal, hearts of palm, and other ingredients that make a beautiful first course or entrée.

¼ cup peanut oil

1 medium-size onion, minced

1 clove garlic, minced

1 tablespoon minced fresh parsley

1 tablespoon minced fresh chives

1 pound jumbo shrimp

Salt and freshly ground black pepper to taste

2 cups water

2 cups cornmeal

One 4-ounce can sardines in oil

¼ pound pitted black olives

¼ pound pimiento-stuffed olives

1 medium-size firm ripe tomato, thinly sliced

2 hard-boiled eggs, peeled and thinly sliced

One 16-ounce can hearts of palm, thinly
    sliced into rounds

1 cabbage leaf

In a large saucepan, heat the oil over medium heat. Add the onion, garlic, parsley, and chives and cook, stirring. When the onions are soft, add the shrimp, salt, pepper, and water. When the shrimp turn pink, cover and cook for 7 minutes. Remove the shrimp, and peel and devein them. Reserve the cooking liquid.

Pour the cornmeal into a bowl. Add the sardines and the reserved cooking liquid from the shrimp. Work the mixture with your hands until you have a paste. Butter the top part of a couscousier or a heavy colander and line it with a thin layer of cheesecloth. Arrange the shrimp, olives, and tomato, egg, and hearts of palm slices around the sides. Fill the rest of the colander with the cornmeal mixture. (If you wish to have a fancy *cuscuz*, you can alternate layers of sliced vegetables and shrimp with the cornmeal mixture.) Fill the lower half of the couscousier, or a pot large enough for the colander to rest on, with water and bring it to a boil. Place the top half back on the couscousier or the colander on the second pot. Traditionally the join is tied with a dishtowel and a cabbage leaf is placed on the top of the *cuscuz*. The *cuscuz* is steamed over medium heat for a half an hour, or until the dishtowel is damp and the cabbage leaf has turned yellow. Allow the *cuscuz* to sit for a few minutes, then unmold it onto a plate. Cut it into serving slices with an oiled knife.

Casquinha de Siri

Brazilian Style Crab Backs

MAKES 4 SERVINGS

This Brazilian appetizer from Rio takes time and energy to prepare, most of which is spent cleaning out the crab shells in which the prepared dish is served. If you have small crab-shaped ceramic dishes that are ovenproof, you can save yourself this effort. If not, scrub away. Traditionally the dish calls for small crabs, which are caught and sold on strings in the open markets. If you live in a West Indian neighborhood, you will occasionally find them at a fish market or even at a greengrocer's. However, this recipe has been adapted for any small crab.

8 small crabs

1 pound crabmeat, flaked and picked over
    for cartilage

Juice of 2 lemons

Salt and freshly ground black pepper to taste

3 tablespoons salted butter

2 medium-size onions, minced

2 cloves garlic, minced

2 medium-size ripe tomatoes, peeled, seeded,
    and coarsely chopped

½ teaspoon minced preserved malagueta
    pepper or to taste (see page 88)

1 medium-size green bell pepper, cored,
    seeded, and minced

1 tablespoon flour

¼ cup freshly grated Parmesan cheese

Cook the crabs by plunging them into a pot of boiling water and cooking them for 8 to 10 minutes. Drain, remove the claws, and pick the meat from the shell, keeping the shells intact.

Place all the crabmeat in a bowl with the lemon juice, salt, and pepper. Allow it to marinate for 20 minutes. Melt the butter in a large saucepan over medium heat, then cook the onions and garlic until they are soft. Gradually add the tomato, malagueta pepper, bell pepper, and the flaked crabmeat which has been removed from its marinade. Cook, stirring occasionally, adding some of the marinade if the mixture seems too dry. Add the flour, reduce the heat to low, and stir until the mixture thickens.

Fill each of the crab shells with the crabmeat mixture and sprinkle some Parmesan cheese on the top. Place the crab shells on an ungreased cookie sheet and cook them in a preheated 350°F oven for 15 minutes, or until the Parmesan has melted and browned. Serve hot.

TEMPEROS E ACOMPANHAMENTOS

Condiments and Accompaniments

ANYONE WHO has ever eaten in a Brazilian restaurant knows that the table rapidly fills up not only with dishes of beans and rice, but also with small plates and wooden bowls brimming with all of the things that Brazilians use to give that certain extra something to their food. These side dishes include bowls of cassava meal called *farinha* (flour) which is toasted and served in a seemingly endless number of ways, sauces called *molhos* which are prepared according to the whim of the cook to go with virtually every recipe in the Brazilian repertoire, and, the big daddy of all Brazilian condiments—pepper.

There are several different types of pepper in Brazil and by pepper I mean chiles. Brazilians avoid this confusion by calling black and white peppercorns *pimenta do reino*, meaning pepper from the kingdom. This is obviously a throwback to the days when all of the peppercorns in Brazil were imported from the mother country, Portugal. However, those days are long over and Brazil grows and processes a respectable amount of the world's black pepper.

The pepper, though, that is for many the hallmark of Brazil's cooking is the malagueta pepper. These tiny peppers are sold fresh and preserved in markets. They appear on virtually every table in the country, and can be summoned at restaurants with the simple word, *pimenta*. For the botanical description of malagueta pepper, see page 48. However, the information there cannot convey the fondness that

Brazilians have for these little incendiary chiles. Along with *pimenta malagueta*, Brazilians also have a fondness for *pimenta de cheiro* ("pepper with a smell"). This lantern-shaped chile seems to be a relative of the superhot habanero and adds not only heat, but also flavor to many dishes from Bahia and all over Brazil. Malagueta madness is a national passion. Specialists called *pimentologos* debate the varieties, health benefits, and uses of Brazil's chiles. Others just eat them. It's always astonishing for first-time visitors to sit in a restaurant and watch a couture-clad lady ask for and eat amazing amounts of chiles without turning a well-coifed hair.

Pimenta Malagueta I

Malagueta Pepper I

———— ◆ ————

MAKES 1½ CUPS

This is the hallmark of most Brazilian cooking. These chiles are similar to the bird and tabasco chiles that can occasionally be found in North American markets. If you are lucky enough to find some fresh and want to prepare them, try this recipe from my friend Marcelo.

> 1 pound pimenta malagueta or bird chiles
>   (see page 48)
>
> 1 cup vodka
>
> 1 sterilized wine bottle
>
> 1 cup extra virgin olive oil
>
> ½ cup vinegar

Spread the bird chiles on a work surface and pick over them, removing any that are blemished or spoiled. Be sure not to touch your face or eyes while working with them. Then place them in a bowl and wash carefully with the vodka. (Water will make them spoil, according to Marcelo.) Dry them carefully with paper towels. Force the chiles into the sterilized wine bottle or into any sterilized glass container that can be stoppered and add the oil and vinegar to cover. (If the measurements given here aren't enough to cover, add more in a 2 to 1 ratio.) Stopper with a cork and allow to rest for a month, away from heat and direct sunlight. When ready, uncork and serve. You can either use the liquid from the chiles or the chiles themselves. Use sparingly unless you're a true chile head. It will keep indefinitely.

Pimenta Malagueta II

Malagueta Pepper II

———— ◆ ————

Not everyone has the time to prepare their own chiles, even in Brazil where they're virtually the staff of life. For those who don't, follow this easy method. Check in your local supermarket or specialty food store or locate a mail-order source on pages 271–272. Write, phone or visit. Select your chiles and voilà, malagueta pepper the easy way.

Molho Simple

Simple Sauce

MAKES ABOUT ½ CUP

This sauce is a household staple in most of Brazil. Cooks add their favorite herbs and a dash of something that makes it just theirs—a bit of minced parsley or coriander, a pinch of minced garlic, a different proportion of oil to vinegar. This though, is the basic recipe. Experiment and come up with a *molho* that is truly yours.

¼ cup oil

1 small onion, thinly sliced

1 small ripe tomato, peeled, seeded, and coarsely chopped

1 tablespoon vinegar

3 black peppercorns

Salt and minced habanero chile to taste (see page 88)

2 tablespoons water

Heat the oil over medium heat in a small saucepan. Add the onion and cook, stirring, until it softens. Add the tomato and vinegar and reduce the heat to low. Add the remaining ingredients, return the heat to medium, and bring the sauce to a boil. Remove it from the heat and chill in the refrigerator for 1 hour. Serve with everything. It will keep in the refrigerator for a month or more.

Molho Campanha

Country Sauce

MAKES ABOUT 2 CUPS

This Brazilian sauce is the perfect accompaniment for grilled steaks and chicken. Its vinegary taste just seems to bring out their flavor. Make only a small batch at a time as this is a sauce which is not going to improve by sitting around, and the vegetables will wilt.

- 2 medium-size firm, ripe tomatoes, peeled, seeded, and coarsely chopped
- 1 large onion, minced
- 1 small green bell pepper, cored, seeded, and minced
- 1 cup red wine vinegar
- 1 teaspoon minced fresh coriander (cilantro)

Place all of the ingredients together in a glass (nonreactive) bowl and stir to mix well. Cover with plastic wrap and store for 1 hour so that the flavors can mix. Serve at room temperature with grilled meat.

Molho Apimentado

Spicy Sauce

MAKES 1½ CUPS

This sauce is the traditional accompaniment to Rio's *feijoada*. It is prepared with the cooking liquid from the *feijoada*'s beans, *molho campanha* (see previous recipe), and as much malagueta pepper as you wish.

> 1 cup Molho Campanha (preceding recipe)
>
> ½ cup cooking liquid from the feijoada's beans (see page 171)
>
> 3 or 4 preserved malagueta peppers, minced, or to taste (see page 88)

Mix all of the ingredients together in a nonreactive bowl and serve at room temperature with the *feijoada*.

Molho de Pimenta e Limão

Chile and Lime Sauce

MAKES ABOUT ½ CUP

This is traditionally served with *Moqueca de Peixe* (see page 197). It's also delicious with grilled meats. This sauce is sometimes called *Molho Carioca* and is also a traditional accompaniment to Rio's *feijoadas* and stews.

> **4 preserved malagueta peppers, minced, or to taste (see page 88)**
>
> **1 teaspoon salt**
>
> **1 small onion, minced**
>
> **1 clove garlic, minced**
>
> **Juice of 3 limes**

Place the malagueta peppers and salt in a mortar and crush them with the pestle or process them in a blender or food processor until you have a thick paste. Gradually add the onion and garlic and continue to mash into the paste. Then add lime juice to the paste, mashing as you do, until you have a liquid sauce. Cover with plastic wrap, allow to stand at room temperature for half an hour, and serve.

Molho Nago

Nago Sauce

MAKES ABOUT ⅔ CUP

Nago is the Bahian term for the descendants of the Yoruba slaves who arrived in that region from southwestern Nigeria and eastern Benin in the eighteenth and nineteenth centuries. By the 1800s, people from this area represented the majority of the slaves in the Bahian region. The cooking of the Yoruba people shows its African origins in its use of malagueta pepper, *dendê*, and okra. It is considered by culinary historians to be one of the most original regional cuisines in all of Brazil. This sauce is traditionally served with stews.

> **4 or 5 preserved malagueta peppers (see page 88)**
>
> ½ **teaspoon salt**
>
> **3 tablespoons crushed dried smoked shrimp (see page 35)**
>
> **6 medium-size okra pods, cooked (see page 150) and cut into rounds**
>
> ⅓ **cup fresh lime juice**

Place the malagueta peppers, salt, shrimp, and okra in a food processor and pulse until you have pureed them. Then gradually add the lime juice and mix until you have a thick liquid. If the sauce is being served with a stew, add a few tablespoons of the stew liquid to the sauce and then serve.

Molho Baiano

Bahian Sauce

MAKES ABOUT ⅓ CUP

One of the hallmarks of the cooking of Bahia is its use of the currently controversial bright orange palm oil which is called *dendê* in Brazil. In this sauce, the *dendê* is flavored with dried smoked shrimp and malagueta peppers.

> **4 preserved malagueta peppers (see page 88)**
>
> **Salt to taste**
>
> **2 tablespoons dried smoked shrimp (see page 35)**
>
> **1 teaspoon minced fresh ginger**
>
> **2 tablespoons dendê (see page 39)**

Place the malagueta peppers and salt in a mortar and pound them into a paste. Add the dried shrimp and ginger and mash until the mixture is a thick uniform paste. Remove the paste from the mortar and place it in a heavy skillet. Add the *dendê* and slowly bring the sauce to a boil over medium heat. Serve the sauce warm in a small bowl to accompany grilled meats and Bahian specialties.

Molho Brasileiro

Brazilian Sauce

MAKES ABOUT ⅓ CUP

This lime-based sauce is so popular in Brazil that it is simply called Brazilian sauce. It is eaten with grilled meats, with roasts, and drizzled over stewed vegetables.

Juice of 3 limes

Salt and freshly ground black pepper to taste

2 teaspoons minced fresh parsley

2 teaspoons minced onion

1 teaspoon minced fresh coriander (cilantro)

Minced preserved malagueta pepper to taste (see page 88)

Place all of the ingredients together in a small glass (nonreactive) bowl. Stir to mix well. Cover with plastic wrap and allow to stand for half an hour for the flavors to mix. Serve at room temperature.

Molho Vinaigrete

Vinaigrette

MAKES ABOUT ½ CUP

This is Brazil's classic sauce to accompany cold meats and fried fish. I happen to think that it is wonderful with just about anything. It's simple to prepare and you can, and should, vary the ingredients to your own taste.

3 tablespoons extra virgin olive oil

1 tablespoon red wine vinegar

1 tablespoon minced red bell pepper

2 teaspoons minced fresh parsley

1 small onion, minced

1 small ripe tomato, peeled, seeded, and minced

Salt and freshly ground black pepper to taste

Mix all of the ingredients together in a small nonreactive bowl, cover, and allow the vinaigrette to sit for half an hour for the flavors to mix. Serve at room temperature.

Molho Rita

Rita's Sauce

MAKES ABOUT ½ CUP

Rita was born in the tiny town across from Cachoeira in the state of Bahia. From her mother she learned how to prepare local specialties at a young age, for she was adopted by my friend Antonio Luiz at age twelve and has grown up in the city of Salvador. A proud housewife and an excellent cook, Rita loves to tutor me in the preparation of Bahian and northeastern specialties. She shows me how to make rich Bahian desserts, how to cook black-eyed peas the Brazilian way, and how to make her special sauce that always appears on the table. The simple sauce has become one of my favorites. It's perfect on everything from grilled meats to salads.

> 1 clove garlic, minced
>
> 1 shallot, minced
>
> 1 small onion, minced
>
> 2 teaspoons minced fresh coriander (cilantro)
>
> Salt and minced preserved malagueta pepper to taste
>
> ⅓ cup red wine vinegar
>
> 2 tablespoons extra virgin olive oil

Place all of the ingredients together in a nonreactive bowl and mix well. Cover with plastic wrap and refrigerate for at least an hour so that the flavors mix. Serve chilled with grilled meats and virtually all Bahian main dishes.

Vinaigrete ao Basilic

Basil Vinaigrette

MAKES ABOUT ¾ CUP

This salad dressing with its taste of garden-fresh basil is perfect on tomato salads made from fresh ripe tomatoes. The basil is a hint of the Italian influence form the southern areas of Brazil around Santa Catarina.

Salt and freshly ground black pepper to taste

1½ tablespoons red wine vinegar

5 tablespoons extra virgin olive oil

1 tablespoon minced fresh basil

½ teaspoon minced garlic

Place the salt and pepper in a small glass (nonreactive) bowl. Add the vinegar and stir until the salt is completely dissolved. Then drizzle in the olive oil, stirring constantly. Finally, add the basil and garlic, continuing to stir. Cover with plastic wrap and allow the vinaigrette to sit for one half hour to let the flavors mix. Serve drizzled over a fresh tomato salad or the salad of your choice.

Molho para Salada

Salaȡ Dreȴȴing

———— ◆ ————

MAKES ABOUT ¾ CUP

This is quite simply a classic vinaigrette salad dressing. In the salad section of the book, you'll find suggestions for ways you can vary this dressing so that it will harmonize with the tastes of various salads. You may, though, simply decide to use it as is on a simple salad of fresh greens and ripe tomatoes.

¼ cup red wine vinegar

Salt and freshly ground black pepper to taste

Pinch of sugar

1 teaspoon minced fresh parsley

¼ teaspoon minced garlic

9 tablespoons extra virgin olive oil

Combine all of the ingredients except the olive oil in a small nonreactive bowl and mix them together well. Gradually drizzle in the oil, continuing to stir until the vinaigrette is well mixed.

Molho Verde

Green Sauce

MAKES ABOUT ⅔ CUP

This is one of my favorite Brazilian salad dressings. For years, the salad dressing at Via Brasil, my favorite Brazilian restaurant in New York, was a mysterious green sauce that everyone, myself included, assumed was avocado. The sauce was rich and creamy with a hint of chile. Imagine my surprise one day when I was told that the salad dressing was prepared from the outside leaves of the lettuce with a hint of malagueta pepper. This is my variation of it.

2 tablespoons minced watercress

2 tablespoons minced fresh parsley

½ cup minced Boston lettuce leaves

3 tablespoons extra virgin olive oil

2 tablespoons fresh lemon juice

1 preserved malagueta pepper or to taste (see
  page 88)

1 tablespoon plain yogurt

Place all of the ingredients into a blender or food processor and mix until you have a thick, frothy liquid. Remove and serve immediately over salads, otherwise it will separate.

Maionese de Kiwi I

Kiwi Mayonnaise I

MAKES 1½ CUPS

This is a fruit mayonnaise that was devised by my São Paulo friend Nair de Carvalho. Nair, who is an artist, was forced to improvise a meal one evening at a gathering of friends. The result was a poached fish that was served with this kiwi mayonnaise. It is delicious with poached fish or with fresh fruit and seafood salads, and naturally with Poached Red Snapper Nair (see page 194). This is the classic way with homemade mayonnaise.

> **2 large egg yolks**
>
> **Salt to taste**
>
> **½ teaspoon ground mustard**
>
> **Pinch of sugar**
>
> **Pinch of cayenne pepper**
>
> **4 teaspoons fresh lemon juice**
>
> **1½ cups extra virgin olive oil**
>
> **4 teaspoons hot water**
>
> **1 kiwi, peeled and minced**

Place the egg yolks, salt, mustard, sugar, cayenne, and three teaspoons of the lemon juice in a blender or food processor and mix it at low speed for 10 seconds. Gradually increase the blender speed while slowly drizzling in the olive oil. As the mixture begins to thicken, continue to add the oil, alternating it with a mixture of the hot water and the remaining lemon juice. When the mayonnaise is prepared, add the minced kiwi and continue to blend for 15 seconds. Chill and serve. It will keep several days in the refrigerator.

Maionese de Kiwi II

Kiwi Mayonnaise II

MAKES ABOUT 1¼ CUPS

Even though it takes very little time to prepare a homemade mayonnaise, we don't all do it. For the lazy ones, myself included at times, here's the quick way with Nair's kiwi mayonnaise.

1 cup mayonnaise

1 kiwi, peeled and minced

Place the mayonnaise and the kiwi in a blender or food processor and pulse for 1 minute until well mixed. Serve chilled.

Farinha

In Brazil cassava, or manioc flour, *farinha de mandioca*, is sometimes served alone on the table after it has been lightly toasted and is used to sprinkle over dishes like *feijoada* (see page 171) or *Tutu a Mineira* (see page 144). The grainy meal adds crunch and the slightly sour taste of cassava to the dish. In Brazil there are frequently shakers of cassava meal on restaurant tables and many Brazilians have ended up with a pizza full of garlic the first time at an American pizzeria because they thought that the shaker was full of *farinha*. If you find untoasted cassava meal, you can toast it by placing a cupful in a heavy cast-iron skillet and cooking it over low heat, stirring constantly, until the meal becomes a beigy brown color, about 5 minutes.

Much *farinha de mandioca* in Brazil is transformed into one type or another of the condiments known as *farofas*. These dishes are prepared in one of three basic ways: 1) by adding water to the *farinha* and then other ingredients; 2) by frying the *farinha* in one of several types of oil; and 3) by adding the *farinha* to a sauce or a group of ingredients. Specialists in the art of making *farofas* are sometimes called *farofeiros* and have been known to prepare as many as 83 different variations on the *farofa* theme. Here are some variations. You can experiment with adding ingredients ranging from small pieces of banana to bits of shredded kale.

Farofa d'Água

Water Farofa

MAKES ABOUT ½ CUP

This is an elaborate variation on the first method of preparing *farofa*.

½ cup cassava meal (see page 31)

1 tablespoon minced green pimiento-stuffed olives

2 teaspoons minced fresh chives

2 teaspoons minced fresh parsley

½ teaspoon minced fresh coriander (cilantro)

1 tablespoon extra virgin olive oil

1 tablespoon white wine

4½ teaspoons warm water

Place all of the ingredients except the warm water in a heavy skillet and cook over medium-low heat for 2 to 3 minutes, or until well blended, stirring occasionally. Gradually add the water, continuing to stir. When all of the liquid has been absorbed, the *farofa d'água* is ready to serve as an accompaniment to meat dishes.

Farofa de Dendê

Palm Oil Farofa

MAKES ABOUT 1 CUP

This is a Bahian example of the second type of *farofa*. Because it is Bahian, it uses palm oil which turns the *farinha* a wonderful saffrony yellow.

> 3 tablespoons dendê (see page 39)
>
> 1 small onion, minced
>
> 1 teaspoon minced fresh parsley
>
> 1 tablespoon ground dried shrimp (see page 35)
>
> Salt and freshly ground black pepper to taste
>
> ½ teaspoon minced preserved malagueta peppers or to taste (see page 88)
>
> ¾ cup cassava meal (see page 31)

Heat the *dendê* in a heavy skillet over medium heat. Add all of the remaining ingredients except the cassava meal and cook them, stirring occasionally with a wooden spoon, until the onions have softened. Then gradually add the cassava meal, continuing to stir and making sure that all of the meal turns bright yellow, about 2 minutes. Remove from the heat, stir with a fork, and serve as an accompaniment to traditional Bahian dishes.

Farofa de Manteiga

Butter Farofa

MAKES 1 CUP

For those who would like to attempt a *farofa* prepared with oil, but who do not want *dendê*, here's one prepared with butter.

> **3 tablespoons butter**
>
> **1 small onion, coarsely chopped**
>
> **¾ cup cassava meal (see page 31)**
>
> **¼ cup minced cooked lingüiça (see page 45) or substitute chorizo**
>
> **Salt and freshly ground black pepper to taste**

Melt the butter in a heavy frying pan over medium heat. Add the onion and cook it until it is soft. Slowly add the cassava meal, stirring constantly, and cook until the meal turns golden, about 2 to 3 minutes. Add the sausage pieces and season to taste. Stir a final time to make sure that all of the ingredients are well mixed and serve. This *farofa* can be served warm or at room temperature.

Farofa Amarela

Yellow Farofa

MAKES ABOUT 1 CUP

This is a simple Bahian *farofa* that goes with virtually everything.

1 cup cassava meal (see page 31)

2 tablespoons dendê (see page 39)

Place all of the ingredients in a heavy cast-iron skillet and cook over low heat, stirring occasionally, until the cassava meal has turned yellow, about 2 minutes. Remove, flake with a fork, and serve.

Farofa do Molho

Mixed Farofa

MAKES 1¼ CUPS

The sauce in this *farofa* is simply a mixture of bacon, tomato, onion, garlic, and parsley.

4 strips bacon, cut into 1-inch pieces

1 medium-size firm ripe tomato, peeled, seeded, and coarsely chopped

1 small onion, minced

1 clove garlic, minced

2 teaspoons minced fresh parsley

3 tablespoons butter

1 cup cassava meal (see page 31)

Fry the bacon bits in a heavy skillet until crisp. Add the remaining ingredients, except the cassava meal, to the pan and cook over medium heat until the onion is soft, stirring occasionally. Gradually add the cassava meal and cook, stirring, until the meal turns golden, about 2 minutes. Remove from the heat and serve warm.

SOPAS E SALADAS

Soups and Salads

WHILE THE Brazilians have inherited a fondness for soups from their Portuguese ancestors, they are not salad lovers. However, with an increasing health consciousness among the young people of Rio and São Paulo, salads are becoming "in." The girl from Ipanema does watch her weight. Salads, though, do appear on tables and are frequently served as first courses. My favorite salad is simply plain hearts of palm, and its thick stalks appear on the table at Marius' every time that I'm in Rio. Marius' is my favorite Rio *churrascaria*. I first became acquainted with the restaurant when invited to a whopping great luncheon with a group of travel writers. Since then, Marius' has become a Rio stop with me. It appeals to my love of grilled food as well as to my love of fresh vegetables. When you arrive, you are tempted with a selection of Brazilian drinks: caipirinhas of many different types, batidas, and of course *whiskey nacional*. You're then given a menu pad and asked to check off what you'd like. After hearts of palm are checked off, I simply allow my fellow diners to do the work with an occasional nod, yes, I'd like chicken. No, we don't have to get the liver. Certainly, we absolutely must have the *picanha*. Marius' serves *rodízio* style, which means that waiters circulate through the restaurant carrying huge swords of meat. They stop at tables and give you a slice of whatever you've ordered as many times as you'd like. In short, Marius' is a carnivore's dream. It's ironic, then, that it is also my favorite salad place because prior to the dance of the waiters, diners are served their choice of corn salad, Russian salad, fresh crisp greens, and other salad ingredients and allowed to make their own salads. I've been to other *churrascarias* in Rio and other parts of Brazil. Some have even adopted the American habit of the salad bar. However, none can serve a salad that is quite as delicious as those of Marius'.

Sopa de Hortelã

Mint Soup

MAKES 4 SERVINGS

Although called mint soup, this could perhaps be more accurately called garlic soup. It's simple to make and delicious, a perfect cool-weather soup. Most of us forget that Rio and São Paulo both have their cold seasons, when women get dressed in suits and wools and sometimes even coats are called for.

> 3 tablespoons olive oil
>
> 4 cloves garlic, put through a garlic press
>
> 8 cups water
>
> 4 sprigs fresh mint, coarsely chopped
>
> Salt and freshly ground black pepper to taste
>
> 4 large eggs
>
> 4 slices French bread, toasted
>
> 4 sprigs fresh mint for garnish

In a medium-size saucepan, heat the oil over medium heat. Add the garlic and cook, stirring, until browned. Add the water, mint, salt, and pepper and bring to a boil, still over medium heat. Break the eggs over the boiling soup, allow them to poach for 1 minute, and then remove the soup from the flame. Ladle the soup into earthenware bowls into which you have placed the slices of French bread and garnish with a sprig of fresh mint.

Canja

Brazilian Style Chicken Soup

MAKES 4 TO 6 SERVINGS

One-half 3- to 4-pound chicken

1 medium-size onion, chopped

4 medium-size ripe tomatoes, peeled, seeded, and coarsely chopped

1 stalk celery, with leaves, chopped

1 sprig fresh parsley, minced

10 cups water

3 large carrots, sliced

½ cup uncooked white rice

Salt and freshly ground black pepper to taste

Place the chicken, onion, tomatoes, celery, and parsley in a large stockpot. Add 8 cups of the water, cover, and bring to a boil. Reduce the heat to low and cook for one hour. Remove the chicken and strip the meat from the bones. Discard the bones. Put the cooking liquid and the vegetables through a food mill or force through a colander to obtain a rich chicken stock. Return the stock to the stockpot. Add the reserved chicken meat, carrots, rice, and remaining water to the pot. Place it on a medium flame and bring to a boil. Reduce the heat to low and let simmer for an additional half hour. Season to taste and serve hot.

Fish Stock

MAKES 2 QUARTS

2 quarts cold water

1 pound fish heads, bones, and trimmings

1 carrot, peeled and minced

1 stalk celery, minced

⅛ teaspoon dry thyme

1 sprig fresh parsley

2 black peppercorns

2 teaspoons salt or to taste

Pour the water into a heavy stockpot and add the fish, carrot, and celery. Prepare a bouquet garni by tying the thyme, parsley, and peppercorns into a piece of cheesecloth. Place the bouquet garni in the pot, cover, and simmer for one hour. Then strain through cheesecloth. The stock can be used at once or frozen for future use.

Sopa de Mariscos

Seafood Soup

MAKES 4 SERVINGS

This seafood soup is Bahian and offers the tastes of that region in its coriander and coconut milk. The trick to remember is not to cook the coconut milk. Remove the pan from the stove just after it has been added. This soup can also be prepared from leftover seafood. In that case, shell the mussels before adding them, and decrease the cooking time to 5 minutes.

¼ pound bay or sea scallops

¼ pound crabmeat

¼ pound mussels, shelled and washed (see note on page 116)

¼ pound shrimp, peeled and deveined (see page 34)

¼ cup pure olive oil

1 small green bell pepper, seeded and sliced into strips

2 small onions, sliced

1 bay leaf

Salt, minced fresh coriander (cilantro), and freshly ground black pepper to taste

5 cups fish stock (see page 114)

½ cup thin coconut milk (see page 38)

Heat the olive oil in a large, heavy skillet over medium heat. Add all of the ingredients except the fish stock and the coconut milk, and cook for 2 to 3 minutes. Add the fish stock and allow it to come to a boil. Then lower the heat, cover, and simmer for ten minutes, or until the mussels have opened. Remove any mussels that have not opened, pour in the coconut milk, stir, and remove the soup from the heat. Serve hot with garlic bread.

NOTE: To prepare the mussels, scrub them with a stiff brush, remove any barnacles, and cut off any beard. Then place them in a bowl of cold water for about 2 hours so that they will purge themselves of sand. When ready to cook, remove them, drain, and discard any that float or are slightly open.

Sopa de Milho

Corn Soup

MAKES 4 SERVINGS

In Brazil this dish is often made with fresh corn which is scraped from the cob. However, it's almost as good and can be made all year round if it's prepared with canned corn, as in this method.

> **One 16-ounce can yellow corn (Green Giant**
> **Niblets are very good), drained, or 2 cups**
> **fresh or frozen corn**
>
> **4 cups milk**
>
> **1 small onion, quartered**
>
> **1 slice white bread, crusts removed**
>
> **Salt and freshly ground black pepper to taste**
>
> **4 small cooked shrimp**
>
> **1 tablespoon minced fresh parsley**

Place all of the ingredients, except the shrimp and parsley, in a blender or food processor and blend until you have a smooth liquid (you may have to do this in batches). Stir to mix the ingredients well and place in a large saucepan. Adjust the seasonings and bring to a boil over medium heat. Remove and serve garnished with the shrimp and a dusting of parsley.

Sopa de Feijão

Bean Soup

MAKES 6 SERVINGS

In any country where they eat as many beans as they do in Brazil, it's inevitable that there would be bean soup. This soup can be prepared from any type of bean. In Brazil the beans most frequently used are black beans, pink beans, and even occasionally black-eyed peas.

1 pound dried black beans

¼ cup pure olive oil

2 cloves garlic, minced

4 cups water

Salt and freshly ground black pepper to taste

Prepare the beans according to the basic bean recipe on page 41. When the beans are cooked, drain them, reserving the cooking liquid. Heat the oil over medium heat in a stockpot. Add the garlic and cook, stirring, until browned. Add the beans. Stir well to make sure that the beans are well flavored with the garlic. Then put the beans through a food mill along with their cooking liquid or pulse in a blender or food processor until smooth. Return the bean mixture to the stockpot and add the water. Season to taste and bring to a boil over medium heat. Serve hot.

Creme de Palmito

Cream of Hearts of Palm

MAKES 4 TO 6 SERVINGS

In sophisticated São Paulo, my favorite vegetable, hearts of palm, turns up in salads, as a vegetable, and also in soup, as in this cream of hearts of palm. Here it's given a bit of a tang with the use of plain yogurt.

**One 16-ounce can hearts of palm, drained
and 1 tablespoon of the liquid reserved**

2 cups chicken stock (recipe follows)

3 teaspoons flour

1 large egg yolk

3 cups water

¾ cup plain yogurt

Salt and freshly ground black pepper to taste

**2 tablespoons minced fresh parsley for
garnish**

Mix the hearts of palm liquid with the chicken stock, flour, and egg yolk, stirring well with a wooden spoon. Cut the hearts of palm into rounds about ¾ inch thick. Pour the stock mixture over the hearts of palm and stir. Place the mixture in a large saucepan, add the water, and cook for 2 to 3 minutes over medium heat. Gradually add the yogurt while stirring constantly. Season and serve hot with a sprinkling of parsley.

Quick Chicken Stock

MAKES ABOUT 5½ CUPS

6 cups water

1½ pounds chicken backs, necks, and wings

1 celery stalk

Salt to taste

4 sprigs fresh parsley

1 bay leaf

¼ teaspoon minced fresh thyme

6 black peppercorns

Place the water and chicken in a large saucepan with the celery stalk and season with salt. Prepare a bouquet garni by placing the remaining ingredients in a piece of cheesecloth and tying it closed. Add the bouquet garni to the pot and bring it to a boil over medium-high heat. Reduce the heat to low and allow it to simmer for 30 minutes. Strain the stock, discarding the bouquet garni and the celery. You may wish to keep the chicken bits for a chicken salad. The stock is ready to use or it can be cooled and frozen for future use.

Sopa de Siri

Crab Soup

Siri are small crabs that are found in marshy areas. They are threaded on strings and sold along roadsides in northeastern Brazil. They are difficult to find in the United States and are only occasionally available in fish and vegetable markets in West Indian neighborhoods. Instead of this small crab, regular lump crabmeat is substituted and used as the base for this creamy soup.

1 clove garlic, minced

Salt and freshly ground black pepper to taste

⅛ teaspoon minced fresh malagueta chile or to taste

1 pound fresh crabmeat, picked over for cartilage

2 tablespoons unsalted butter

1 medium-size onion, minced

6 cups chicken stock (see page 119)

½ cup light cream or half-and-half

Mix the garlic, salt, pepper, and malagueta pepper together and rub them through the crabmeat. Cover the mixture with plastic wrap and set it aside for 15 minutes. Meanwhile, melt the butter in a large, heavy saucepan over medium heat. When it foams, add the onion and cook, stirring, till they are translucent. Do not allow them to brown. Add the crabmeat and cook, stirring gently, over low heat for 10 minutes. Add the stock and adjust the seasonings, and bring to a boil over medium heat. Add the cream, and serve hot.

Sopa de Coco

Coconut Soup

MAKES 4 TO 6 SERVINGS

The first thing you learn about coconut in Brazil is that if you are not a native Portuguese speaker, it's very important where you put the accent. It belongs on the first syllable — KOH koh. If it's placed on the last syllable, as some English speakers do, it means something quite rude. Anyhow, that over, you can begin to order things with coconut in them without getting strange stares and giggles from waiters. One of the things that you might wish to order is this wonderful coconut soup which is a perfect first course and can become heartier with the addition of any number of garnishes, ranging from minced scallions to cooked shrimp.

> 2 teaspoons cornstarch
>
> 1 cup milk
>
> 2 cups thick coconut milk (see page 38)
>
> 3 cups chicken stock (see page 119)
>
> 1 medium-size onion, minced
>
> Salt and ground allspice to taste
>
> 1 cup light cream or half-and-half
>
> 2 tablespoons minced ham
>
> 2 tablespoons chopped cashew nuts

Blend the cornstarch together with ¼ cup of the milk in a small bowl and reserve. Then place the remaining milk, the coconut milk, chicken stock, onion, salt, and allspice in a large, heavy saucepan and stir well. Heat the mixture over a medium flame until it almost comes to a boil. Gradually add the cornstarch-and-milk mixture, stirring until the soup is smooth and thick. Add the cream, stir, and continue to cook. Do not bring the soup to a second boil. Serve hot, garnished with the chopped ham and cashews.

Palmito

Hearts of Palm

MAKES 2 SERVINGS

Hearts of palm have to be numbered among my favorite salad ingredients. There's something about the texture and flavor of these pieces of palm that have been marinated in brine. In Brazil, where they are run-of-the-mill ordinary, they are inexpensive. Here, though, they are usually only found canned and are definitely a delicacy. I love it when they're called hearts of palm as well. Somehow they don't taste as good when they're called swamp cabbage, as they are in parts of Florida. Anyhow, with things that I adore, I always find that the simplest way is usually the best, so here's the ideal (and expensive) way to serve them à la Marius'.

One 16-ounce can hearts of palm, drained

Check the hearts of palm to see if any have tough outside pieces; if so, cut them off. Place them on a small salad plate, chill, and serve.

Salada de Palmito

Hearts of Palm Salad

MAKES 4 TO 6 SERVINGS

This way with hearts of palm stretches them slightly, but still keeps their tangy taste. It's better when you have a larger group to serve.

One 16-ounce can hearts of palm, drained and cut into 1-inch pieces

½ head romaine lettuce, torn into bite-size pieces

1 small onion, thinly sliced

⅓ cup Molho para Salada (see page 100)

Liquid from a bottle of malagueta peppers to taste (see page 88)

Place the hearts of palm and lettuce in a large salad bowl. Add the onion and pour on the vinaigrette which you have spiced with the liquid from the malagueta peppers. Place in the refrigerator until chilled, toss, and serve.

Salada de Quiabo I

Okra Salad I

MAKES 4 SERVINGS

Okra is one of Africa's gifts to Brazilian cooking. It turns up in many Afro-Bahian dishes. Those who are still unused to okra's slipperiness may wish to meet the little green pods first in a salad with a piquant dressing.

> **6 cups water**
>
> **½ pound small unblemished okra pods, topped and tailed**
>
> **1 small head Boston lettuce, separated into leaves**
>
> **¼ cup Molho para Salada (see page 100)**
>
> **2 teaspoons minced onion**
>
> **¼ teaspoon minced garlic**
>
> **Liquid from a bottle of malagueta peppers to taste (see page 88)**

Bring the water to a boil in a large saucepan. Plunge the okra into the boiling water and cook for 2 to 3 minutes. Remove, drain under cold running water, and pat dry. Place the lettuce leaves in a glass salad bowl and the okra on top of them. Mix the *molho para salada,* onion, garlic, and liquid from the malagueta peppers together, and pour on top of the okra and lettuce. Serve.

Salada de Quiabo II

Okra Salad II

MAKES 4 SERVINGS

This is another way with okra which is for okra lovers only because the slipperiness of the okra simply becomes a part of the salad dressing. It is delicious, though, and has even converted some first-time okra experimenters into okra enthusiasts.

> 6 cups water
>
> 1 pound small unblemished okra pods, topped and tailed
>
> 1 tablespoon minced onion
>
> 1 clove garlic, minced
>
> 3 small preserved malagueta peppers, minced, or to taste (see page 88)
>
> ¼ cup Molho para Salada (see page 100)

Bring the water to a boil in a large saucepan and plunge the okra into it. Allow the okra to cook for 2 to 3 minutes. Remove, drain under cold running water, and pat dry. Add the onion, garlic, and malagueta peppers to the *molho para salada* and mix well. Pour the dressing over the okra and serve warm.

Salada de Xuxu

Chayote Salad

MAKES 4 SERVINGS

The pastel green squash called *xuxu* (shoo-shoo) in Brazil is best known to us by its Mexican name, chayote. They are readily available in supermarkets and are particularly good when served as a vegetable (see page 143) or in salads.

2 chayote, peeled, seeded, and cut into pieces

2 cups water

1 clove garlic, sliced

Salt and freshly ground black pepper to taste

1 hard-boiled egg, shelled and chopped

¼ cup Vinaigrete ao Basilic (see page 99)

1 tablespoon minced fresh parsley

Place the chayote pieces into a medium-size saucepan with the water, garlic, salt, and pepper and cook for about 5 minutes, or until fork tender. Remove them, drain, and place in a glass salad bowl. Cover with plastic wrap and chill in the refrigerator for 1 hour. Add the chopped hard-boiled egg to the *vinaigrete ao basilic*. When ready to serve, pour the dressing over the chayote and sprinkle with the fresh parsley.

Salada de Agrião

Watercress Salad

MAKES 4 SERVINGS

Rita is an almost picture-postcard Brazilian. Blessed with dark, flashing eyes and a smile that lights up the kitchen, she's a good friend and is always ready to give a hand in the kitchen or share a recipe. On a recent trip to Brazil, we spent a morning in the kitchen trading recipes and kitchen hints. One of the first recipes that I asked her for was the recipe for the watercress salad that we had eaten the night before. It was wonderful, with watercress, tomatoes, and shallotlike onions fresh from the family garden.

> **2 bunches fresh watercress**
>
> **1 large ripe tomato, cut into chunks**
>
> **1 small onion, thinly sliced and separated into rings**
>
> **¼ cup Vinaigrete ao Basilic (see page 99)**
>
> **1 teaspoon Molho Rita or to taste (see page 98)**

Wash the watercress thoroughly and cut off any long stems. Pat dry with paper towels. Mix the watercress, tomato, and onion together well on a small platter. Mix the *vinaigrete* and *molho rita* together and drizzle them over the salad.

Salada Rita

Rita's Salad

MAKES 4 SERVINGS

In this unusual salad, Rita uses peanuts to add crunch to avocado and orange. There's also a bit of orange juice added to the vinaigrette to carry through the orangy taste.

> 1 large ripe avocado, peeled, pitted, and cubed
>
> 2 oranges, peeled and sectioned, with the membrane removed
>
> 1 tablespoon fresh orange juice
>
> ¼ cup Vinaigrete ao Basilic (see page 99)
>
> 1 tablespoon crushed peanuts or to taste

Arrange the avocado cubes and orange segments on a small nonreactive platter or in a glass bowl. Mix together the orange juice and *vinaigrete*, and pour it over the salad. Garnish with the crushed peanuts and serve.

Salada de Abacate

Avocado Salad

MAKES 4 SERVINGS

No country could grow avocados as beautiful as Brazil and not use them in salads. This, though, is a new use for the avocado. It is still more often served traditionally with sugar as a dessert (see pages 235, 237). However, with the new diet-conscious generation, the avocado is making its appearance as a salad ingredient as well.

2 large ripe avocados

16 medium-size cooked shrimp, coarsely chopped (see page 34)

¼ cup Vinaigrete ao Basilic (see page 99)

1 tablespoon minced fresh parsley for garnish

Cut the avocados in half lengthwise and remove the pit. Then hollow out the avocados, leaving about ¼ inch of the meat in the shell. Coarsely chop the avocado meat that you have removed. Mix the avocado meat with the chopped shrimp and replace the mixture in the avocado shell. Drizzle on a bit of the *vinaigrete* and garnish with minced parsley.

Salada de Milho

Corn Salad

As with the *Sopa de Milho,* (page 116) this can be made from fresh cooked corn that has been scraped off of the cob. However, a quick way to do this uses canned corn. It's almost as good.

> **One 16-ounce can yellow corn (Green Giant Niblets are very good), drained and 2 tablespoons of the liquid reserved**
>
> **⅓ cup minced red bell pepper**
>
> **⅓ cup minced green bell pepper**
>
> **⅓ cup minced onion**
>
> **⅓ cup Molho para Salada (see page 100)**

Mix the corn, bell peppers, and onions together in a glass salad bowl. Mix together the *molho para salada* and reserved corn liquid and pour over the salad. Cover with plastic wrap and chill for one hour. Serve cold.

Salada de Tomate

Tomato Salad

MAKES 4 SERVINGS

Brazil is one of the countries where tomato lovers can still find firm, vine-ripened, red, tasty tomatoes. When they're available they form the basis for this tomato salad that is simple and delicious, and easy to prepare.

> 4 medium-size firm, ripe tomatoes
>
> 2 medium-size onions, thinly sliced
>
> Salt and freshly ground black pepper to taste
>
> 1 clove garlic, minced
>
> ¼ cup Vinaigrete ao Basilic (see page 99)

Arrange the tomatoes and onion on a small nonreactive platter. Season to taste. Mix together the garlic and *vinaigrete* and drizzle over the tomatoes and onions. Serve immediately.

Salada Mixta

Mixed Salad

MAKES 6 SERVINGS

Brazilians are not big salad eaters, it's true. However, when they pull out all the stops with a mixed salad it's definitely got something in it for almost everyone. After all, it's only natural in a country where fresh vegetables run the gamut from hearts of palm to asparagus and broccoli to collards.

> 1 small head Boston lettuce, torn into
>   bite-size pieces
>
> 1 small head romaine lettuce, torn into
>   bite-size pieces
>
> 2 medium-size ripe tomatoes, sliced
>
> 1 medium-size onion, thinly sliced
>
> 6 pieces hearts of palm, cut into rounds
>
> 1 small green bell pepper, seeded and cut into
>   strips
>
> ⅓ cup Vinaigrete ao Basilic (see page 99)
>
> Salt and freshly ground black pepper to taste

Place the lettuces in a glass salad bowl. Add all the remaining vegetables, except the *vinaigrete,* and mix well. Pour on the *vinaigrete* and mix again and season to taste. Serve immediately.

Salada de Arroz

Rice Salad

MAKES 4 SERVINGS

In a country where rice is so much a part of the daily diet it's not surprising that there would be a salad use for leftover rice. This salad calls for cooked rice, pimiento, onion, and green pepper.

2 cups cooked white rice

4 teaspoons minced pimiento

¼ cup minced green bell pepper

¼ cup minced onion

¼ cup Molho para Salada (see page 100)

Salt and freshly ground black pepper to taste

Mix the rice, pimiento, bell pepper, and onion together in a glass salad bowl. Pour the *molho para salada* over them. Season to taste, then cover with plastic wrap and refrigerate for 1 hour. Serve cold.

VERDURAS, LEGUMES, E FÉCULA

Vegetables and Starches

BELÉM IS a city in the northeastern Brazilian state of Pará at the mouth of the Amazon. It is a city of steaming heat, of riverboats, and of the blocks-long open air market known as the Ver-O-Paso. A stroll through the Ver-O-Paso market, and it is impossible not to want to linger, reveals the scope of this market which is the marketplace for not only the city of Belém, but for numerous known and unknown stops up and down the Amazon. Some stands sell beads, ironwork, and other articles for use in Brazil's African religions. Others offer handmade bird and animal cages created from reeds and bamboo, some of them already inhabited by brightly plumed Amazonian birds and tiny trembling monkeys. Others function as ship chandlers and offer steel fittings, anchors, and rope in every size and shape imaginable. For any lover of food, though, the stands that are the most fascinating are those that display the wide array of Amazonian fruit.

I stopped in Belém on a cruise on one of Sun Line's ships and the contrast between the cacophony of the marketplace and the quiet hum aboard ship was the first thing that struck me. Then I was fascinated by the fruits. There were many familiar ones, but even they seemed to have changed size and shape. Bananas appeared to have grown, shrunk, and changed colors. They appeared in reds, deep purples, all hues of green, as well as the remembered yellows.

There was my favorite passion fruit in both the wrinkled purple and smooth yellow varieties and the also-familiar pineapples and mangoes. I began to falter at the sight of guavas, carambolas or star fruit, and cashew fruit, which I can only identify when it has its distinctive crescent-shaped cashew nut attached. Then there were soursops, sapodillas, kaki, and fruits that are known to me only by their Brazilian names of *jenipapo* and *umbu*, both of which make wonderful juices and delicious fruit liqueurs. The vegetable section of the market was as vast and as varied. It offered breadfruit, hearts of palm, chayotes—called *xuxu*—green eggplantlike *jilo*, prickly *maxixie*, many root vegetables like cassava, beans of every conceivable type, and a wide array of leafy greens.

It is indeed ironic that with the natural bounty that they have been blessed with, Brazilians are not natural vegetable eaters. The country is one in which stews and the meat-and-potato ethic predominate for those who can afford it. This, though, is changing and a friend of mine who had visited a diet doctor in Rio was given a list of everything she could eat as much of as she liked. The list started off with hearts of palm, a delicacy to those of us in northern climes. She complained and I sighed thinking that with hearts of palm, even I might learn to love a diet.

The vegetables and starches of Brazil traditionally accompany or are found cooked with meats, served au gratin, and buried under sauces. Increasingly today, they are being cooked simply—boiled or steamed and topped with savory sauces. Whichever way, the heartiness of the past or the "lite" taste of the future, they are one of the examples of the country's culinary wealth.

Abóbora Refogada

Stewed Pumpkin

MAKES 4 SERVINGS

Pumpkin is served as a vegetable and as a dessert in Brazil. The pumpkin that is most frequently used is the one known here as calabaza, or the West Indian cooking pumpkin. In this recipe the pumpkin is stewed with garlic, scallions, and chile to make a very different pumpkin taste from the sweetened orange filling that we put into our Thanksgiving pies.

> **1 pound calabaza, seeded, peeled, and cut into pieces (see page 28)**
>
> **2 tablespoons salted butter**
>
> **1 clove garlic, minced**
>
> **2 scallions, minced, including some of the green tops**
>
> **Minced habanero chile to taste (see page 49)**

Place the calabaza into a medium-size saucepan with the butter, garlic, and scallions over medium heat and cook, stirring, until the butter has melted. Cover, reduce the heat to low, and cook for 10 minutes, or until the pumpkin is fork tender. Stir the mixture occasionally so that it does not stick. Uncover the saucepan, check the seasonings, and add the minced chile. Continue to cook for an additional 3 to 5 minutes and then serve warm.

Quibebe de Abóbora Baiana

Bahian Pumpkin Puree

MAKES 6 SERVINGS

This is another way to prepare pumpkin; here it is a puree. This recipe is from the northeastern Brazilian state of Bahia which has the reputation for having some of the country's best and most sophisticated cooking.

> 2 pounds calabaza, seeded, peeled, and
> coarsely chopped (see page 28)
>
> ¼ cup water
>
> 2 tablespoons pure olive oil
>
> 1 teaspoon minced fresh basil
>
> 1 teaspoon sugar
>
> 2 teaspoons beef bouillon
>
> Salt and freshly ground black pepper to taste

Place the pumpkin in a large saucepan with the water, cover, and cook for 10 minutes, or until the pumpkin is fork tender. Meanwhile, heat the olive oil over medium heat in a large saucepan, then add the basil and cook, stirring, for 2 to 3 minutes. When the pumpkin is cooked, puree it in a food mill, blender, or food processor and add it to the basil. Cook for 2 to 3 minutes, then add the sugar, bouillon, salt, and pepper. Continue to cook for an additional 3 minutes. Serve hot.

Alcachofras Cozidas

Boiled Artichokes

───────── ◆ ─────────

MAKES 4 SERVINGS

It might seem unusual to find boiled artichokes in a Brazilian cookbook. However, in Rio and in São Paulo, these globes are indeed served hot or cold as vegetables and accompanied by the various savory sauces that the Brazilians prepare to go with their meats and vegetables.

4 medium-size artichokes

¼ cup cider vinegar

Juice of 3 lemons

2 teaspoons salt

Prepare the artichokes by cutting off the fibrous stem and snipping the points off the leaves with kitchen shears. Wash them thoroughly in water to which the cider vinegar has been added. When finished, leave them in a mixture of the lemon juice and water to cover so they won't darken. When ready to cook, place them in a medium-size saucepan with enough water to cover, bring to a boil, and let boil over medium heat until they are soft, about 35 minutes. Remove, drain, and allow to chill in the refrigerator for several hours. Serve cold with *Molho Vinaigrete* (page 97).

Couve a Mineira

Greens Mineira Style

MAKES 6 TO 8 SERVINGS

This side dish traditionally accompanies *Feijoada* (page 171) and dishes from the northeastern region of Minas Gerais. However, for those who are looking for a new way with green vegetables, it becomes a vegetable dish. This can be prepared with broccoli rabe or green cabbage, but my favorite way is with kale, or *couve*.

> **2 pounds fresh kale (see page 39)**
>
> **3 tablespoons pure olive oil**
>
> **1 medium-size onion, minced**
>
> **2 cloves garlic, minced**

Wash the kale thoroughly and bunch it together. Take each bunch, roll it tightly, and cut it crosswise into thin strips. Wash the strips and drain them thoroughly. Heat the oil in a large, heavy skillet over medium heat, then cook the onion and garlic, stirring them until they are lightly browned. Add the kale strips and cook, stirring, for 5 minutes so that the greens are soft, but retain their bright green color. Serve hot.

Xuxu com Molho

Chayote with Sauce

MAKES 6 SERVINGS

The pastel green squash that is known as the chayote in many parts of the United States is called the *xuxu* (pronounced shoo-shoo) in Brazil. It turns up in stews, salads, and served in several ways as a vegetable. The virtue of the blandly flavored *xuxu* is that it takes on the flavor of the ingredients with which it is prepared. For this reason, it is wonderful when served chilled with a lemony hot sauce.

4 medium-size chayote, peeled, seeded, and cut into slices (see page 53)

½ cup water

Place the chayote in a large saucepan with the water. Cover and cook over low heat for 10 minutes, or until fork tender. Remove from the heat, drain, and chill in the refrigerator for 2 hours. Arrange the pieces on a platter and drizzle them with *Molho de Pimenta e Limão* (see page 93). Serve cold.

Bambu

Bamboo Shoots

MAKES 4 SERVINGS

Bamboo shoots would seem to be an unusual ingredient in Brazilian cooking. However, they are eaten chilled covered with a vinaigrette salad dressing in São Paulo where a sizable Japanese population gives many dishes an Asian flavor.

One 8-ounce can bamboo shoots, drained and rinsed well under running water

¼ cup water

Place the bamboo shoots in a small saucepan with the water over medium heat, cover, and cook for 7 minutes, or until the shoots are fork tender. Remove, drain, and serve warm with *Molho Apimentado* (page 92).

Tutu a Mineira

Black Beans Mineira Style

MAKES 4 TO 6 SERVINGS

Although the dish *Tutu a Mineira* is from the northeastern Brazilian province of Minas Gerais, it is easy to make the day after you prepare a *Feijoada* (page 171) using the leftover black beans. The creamed beans are the *tutu*. They are traditionally served with *Couve a Mineira* (page 142) and with fried pork chops, bacon, and fried pieces of lingüiça sausage.

> ¼ **pound streaky slab bacon, cut into 1-inch**
>   **pieces**
>
> 1 **medium-size onion, chopped**
>
> 1 **clove garlic, minced**
>
> 3 **cups drained cooked black beans (see**
>   **page 41)**
>
> **Salt and freshly ground black pepper to taste**
>
> 1 **cup cassava meal (see page 31)**

Fry the bacon bits in a heavy skillet until crisp. Remove and drain on paper towels. Cook the onion and garlic in the bacon fat over medium heat until they are golden. Add the beans, stir well, and season to taste. Reduce the heat to low and slowly add the cassava meal, stirring until the mixture thickens. To serve, pour the *tutu* onto a platter and decorate it with the reserved bacon pieces.

Virado de Feijão

Creamed Beans

MAKES 4 TO 6 SERVINGS

This is another of Brazil's ways with leftover beans. This one, though, is one that will win the appreciation of vegetarians as it does not call for any meat. Although this *virado* does not use any pork or meat products, it is traditionally served with fried sausages, grilled pork chops, or fried eggs.

3 tablespoons olive oil

1 tablespoon minced fresh parsley

1 tablespoon minced fresh chives

1 clove garlic, minced

1 medium-size onion, chopped

Salt and freshly ground black pepper to taste

3 cups drained cooked black beans, cooking
   liquid reserved (see page 41)

1 cup cassava meal (see page 31)

Heat the oil in a heavy skillet over medium heat, then cook the herbs, garlic, and onion, stirring them until the onion is golden. Season, then add the beans and cooking liquid. Allow the beans to cook over low heat for 2 to 3 minutes. Then slowly drizzle in the cassava meal, stirring well until the mixture thickens. Serve hot.

Feijão com Leite de Coco

Black Beans with Coconut Milk

MAKES 4 SERVINGS

Black beans are one of the hallmarks of the cooking of northeastern Brazil. Here they are cooked with coconut milk and finished with a drizzle of *dendê* (palm oil). The result is a souplike dish that incorporates the tastes of the country's coastal north.

3 cups drained cooked black beans, ¼ cup
   cooking liquid reserved (see page 41)

Salt and freshly ground black pepper to taste

¼ cup thin coconut milk (see page 38)

2 tablespoons dendê (see page 39)

Warm the beans in their liquid and put them through a blender or food processor until they are liquefied. Season and place in a medium-size saucepan and cook, stirring occasionally, over low heat until it thickens, 5 to 7 minutes. Add the coconut milk, and continue to cook, stirring occasionally, until the mixture begins to boil. When ready to serve, place the beans in a tureen or individual soup dishes and drizzle a bit of *dendê* that has been heated on top.

Arroz de Viúva

Widow's Rice

MAKES 6 TO 8 SERVINGS

Prepared with thin coconut milk, this dish traditionally accompanies fish and seafood dishes in Bahia. If more coconut milk and sugar are added, it is transformed into a dessert very similar to *Arroz Doce* (see page 224).

3⅓ cups thin coconut milk (see page 38)

1½ cups long-grain rice

½ teaspoon salt

Bring the coconut milk to a boil in a medium-size saucepan. Stir in the rice and salt. Cover, reduce the heat to low and simmer for 20 minutes. Remove the rice from the heat and allow it to stand for 5 minutes, or until all of the liquid has been absorbed. Serve hot.

Arroz de Hauça

Hausa Rice

MAKES 6 TO 8 SERVINGS

No one is really sure exactly how Hausa rice got its name. However, the Hausa people from northern Nigeria were enslaved in Brazil during the colonial period. In fact, during the period from 1805 to 1835, the Hausa represented one of the three major African groups in the city of Bahia. The Hausa are traditionally Islamic peoples and this rice is prepared with the preserved beef that is known as *charque* or *carne seca*. For those who cannot find *carne seca*, a non-Islamic version can be made with streaky slab bacon.

½ pound carne seca or streaky slab bacon (see page 36)

3⅓ cups water

1½ cups long-grain rice

1 teaspoon salt

1 tablespoon olive oil

1 medium-size onion, sliced

1 clove garlic, minced

Soak the *carne seca* in several changes of water for 24 hours in the refrigerator to remove the saltiness. Then, cut into small pieces. If using bacon, just cut into small pieces.

Bring the water to a boil in a medium-size saucepan. Stir in the rice and salt, cover, and simmer over low heat for 25 minutes. Remove the rice from the heat and allow it to stand for 5 minutes, or until all of the water has been absorbed.

Fry the diced *carne seca* in the oil in a heavy medium-size skillet over medium-high heat until it is browned. (Eliminate the oil if using bacon.) Remove the meat and drain it on paper towels. Add the onion and garlic to the drippings and cook, stirring, over medium heat until they are soft, but not browned. Add the onion-and-garlic mixture to the *carne seca,* then pour the mixture over the rice. Serve hot to accompany traditional Bahian dishes.

Arroz com Camarões

Rapid Rice with Shrimp

MAKES 4 SERVINGS

Brazilians have a number of ways of fixing the rice that is such an important part of their daily diets. Inventive chefs create dishes using whatever is in their larders. This is just such a dish that uses cooked rice and shrimp as well as fresh tomatoes, onions, and garlic.

> **2 tablespoons pure olive oil**
>
> **1 large ripe tomato, peeled, seeded, and coarsely chopped**
>
> **1 small onion, minced**
>
> **1 clove garlic, minced**
>
> **2 cups cooked white rice (see page 31)**
>
> **8 cooked medium-size shrimp (see page 34)**
>
> **Salt, freshly ground black pepper, and minced habanero chile (see page 49) to taste**

Heat the oil in a heavy, large skillet over medium heat. Add the tomato, onion, and garlic and cook, stirring, until the onion is translucent. Add the rice and shrimp and stir well. Season and cook over low heat until the ingredients are heated through. Serve hot.

Quiabo

Okra

MAKES 4 SERVINGS

Wherever okra is seen, Africa has passed through. The tiny green pods are indigenous to Africa and came to the New World both north and south with the slaves. In Africa okra is prized for its thickening properties. In much of the New World, though, these properties are avoided. This is an easy dish in which the okra is simply blanched. It can only be prepared when the okra pods are small and tender.

2 cups water

**1 pound small unblemished okra pods, topped
and tailed**

Place the water in a large saucepan and bring it to a boil over medium heat. Plunge the okra into the water and allow it to cook for 3 to 5 minutes. Remove the okra, drain, and serve hot with a pat of butter.

Quiabos Cozidos

Stewed Okra

It seems that throughout the New World okra meets up with tomatoes and onions. The spices change according to the taste of the land, but okra, onions, and tomatoes are constants. Here, then, is a Brazilian variation on the theme.

> 1 pound small unblemished okra, topped and
> tailed
>
> 2 large ripe tomatoes, peeled, seeded, and
> coarsely chopped
>
> 1 large onion, coarsely chopped
>
> 1 cup water
>
> 1 teaspoon minced fresh basil
>
> 1 teaspoon minced habanero chile (see
> page 49)
>
> Salt and freshly ground black pepper to taste

Place all of the ingredients in a large saucepan and cook over medium heat for 10 minutes, or until the okra is fork tender and the tastes have mixed. Serve hot.

Vagems com Alecrim e Manjericão

String Beans with Rosemary and Basil

MAKES 4 TO 6 SERVINGS

The herbal tastes of cooler climates come into play in Brazil in dishes such as this. Here fresh rosemary and basil season the string beans along with the more traditional garlic and onion.

6 cups water

1 pound firm unblemished string beans, tips removed

3 tablespoons salted butter

¼ teaspoon minced garlic

3 tablespoons minced onion

1 teaspoon minced fresh rosemary

1 teaspoon minced fresh basil

Place the water in a large saucepan and bring it to a boil over high heat. Plunge the string beans in the boiling water and cook them for 3 minutes. Remove from heat, rinse with cold water, and drain. Meanwhile, melt the butter in a heavy large skillet over medium heat, add the remaining ingredients and cook, stirring, until the onion is soft. Add the string beans and cook for 2 to 3 minutes, stirring to make sure that the string beans are coated with the oniony herb butter.

Batata Doce Frita

Fried Sweet Potatoes

When regular french fries get a little ordinary, Brazilian cooks make french fries from the wonderful sweet potatoes they have. They are not as orangy as the ones that most of us are familiar with and can be found in Hispanic markets as *batatas dulces*. They are usually eaten with pork dishes, but I find they're great with everything.

Vegetable oil for frying

3 large sweet potatoes, peeled and cut into lengthwise strips

2 tablespoons kosher salt

Heat 4 to 5 inches of oil to 375°F over medium-high heat in a large fryer or heavy cast-iron saucepan. Rub the potato strips with the salt and place them a few at a time in the hot oil. Fry until they are lightly browned, 2 to 3 minutes. Remove them with a slotted spoon and drain on paper towels. Serve hot.

Bobó de Inhame

Bahian Yam Dish

MAKES 6 SERVINGS

In the United States there is eternal confusion over what is a yam. Botanically, a true yam is a hairy tuber that can attain prodigious length and weight. (The largest ever recorded weighed almost a quarter of a ton!!) They are typical of the cooking of West Africa and of many places in the New World including Brazil. This dish is typical of the country's northeastern region, calling for dried smoked shrimp, ginger, and *dendê* (palm oil). It is traditionally served as an accompaniment for fish or meat dishes.

> **One 1-pound yam, quartered (see page 43)**
>
> **4½ teaspoons dendê (see page 39)**
>
> **¼ cup ground dried smoked shrimp (see page 35)**
>
> **1 small onion**
>
> **1 clove garlic, minced**
>
> **½ teaspoon minced fresh ginger**
>
> **½ teaspoon minced preserved malagueta or fresh habanero chile (see page 49)**
>
> **Salt to taste**
>
> **½ pound cooked shrimp (see page 34)**

Place the yam in a large saucepan with water to cover, and cook over medium heat until tender, about 30 minutes. When ready, remove the yam and drain it. Peel the yam and put it through a food mill or puree it in a blender or food processor. Meanwhile, heat the *dendê* in a heavy skillet over low heat. Add the ground shrimp, onion, garlic, ginger, chile, and salt and cook for 5 to 8 minutes, stirring to keep the ingredients from sticking. Add the whole shrimp and continue to cook until the shrimp are heated through. Gradually add the mashed yam, a spoonful at a time, stirring constantly. Cook the mixture for an additional 5 to 8 minutes, or until it becomes firm. Serve hot.

Milho Verde com Queijo

Creamed Corn Brazilian Style

MAKES 4 SERVINGS

This Brazilian-style creamed corn mixes eggs with fresh corn cut off the cob and Parmesan cheese. Combining a fresh vegetable with cheese and eggs is typical of the Brazilian way with vegetables. A similar dish can be prepared from hearts of palm.

> 5 large egg whites
>
> 2 large egg yolks, lightly beaten
>
> 1 cup heavy cream
>
> ½ cup freshly grated Parmesan cheese
>
> Salt, freshly ground black pepper, and
> ground nutmeg to taste
>
> 1 cup fresh corn cut off the cob

Preheat the oven to 450°F. Place the egg whites in a large mixing bowl and beat until they form stiff peaks. Fold in the two egg yolks, then slowly pour in the cream while continuing to beat. Add the Parmesan and the seasonings, then fold in the corn. Place in individual oiled ramekins and cook for 8 to 10 minutes, or until golden brown on the top. Serve hot.

Omeleta de Camarão

Shrimp Omelette

MAKES 4 SERVINGS

In the coastal areas of Brazil, shrimp are so common that they are used in salads, soups, as appetizers, and even in omelettes. This shrimp omelette can be served as a side dish or by itself with a salad as a light lunch.

6 large eggs

¼ cup heavy cream

¼ cup grated Parmesan cheese

3 tablespoons salted butter

½ cup diced cooked shrimp (see page 34)

Salt and freshly ground black pepper to taste

Break the eggs into a large mixing bowl and beat them well with a whisk. Slowly drizzle in the cream, and mix in the Parmesan cheese. Meanwhile, melt half of the butter in a large heavy skillet over medium heat, add the shrimp bits, and brown them. Add them to the egg mixture. Melt the remaining butter in the skillet over medium heat and when it foams, add the egg-and-shrimp mixture. When the omelette is firm on the outside and slightly runny on the inside, flip it onto a serving dish, folding it over on itself.

Moqueca aos Ovos

Egg Moqueca

Moquecas are savory palm-oil–flavored stews from the northeastern region of Brazil. The most traditional *moquecas* are prepared with fish and shellfish from the coastal waters. This one, though, is a vegetarian egg *moqueca* which is served with white rice.

12 large eggs

3 tablespoons pure olive oil

2 cloves garlic, minced

3 medium-size onions, thinly sliced

2 teaspoons minced fresh coriander (cilantro)

2 tablespoons dendê (see page 39)

Salt and freshly ground black pepper to taste

Break the eggs into a bowl and stir. Meanwhile, heat the oil in a large, heavy skillet over medium heat and cook the garlic, onion, and coriander, stirring, until they are lightly browned. Then pour the eggs into the skillet, stir, and cook for a few seconds. Drizzle in the palm oil, reduce the heat to low, and continue to cook, stirring occasionally, for 5 minutes. Season and serve hot.

Ensopado de Palmito

Stewed Hearts of Palm

MAKES 4 SERVINGS

Hearts of palm are one of the delights of Brazilian cuisine where they are used in a variety of ways, from salads to soufflés. This simple preparation serves them warm with a drizzle of beef stock that enhances the flavor.

> 1 tablespoon salted butter
>
> 1 medium-size onion, thinly sliced
>
> One 16-ounce can hearts of palm, drained,
>   any tough sections removed, and cut into
>   1-inch pieces
>
> ¼ cup Brazilian Beef Stock (recipe follows)

Melt the butter in a medium-size heavy skillet over medium heat and cook the onion, stirring, until it is translucent. Add the hearts of palm pieces and drizzle on the beef stock. Stir and continue to cook until the hearts of palm are heated through. Serve hot with white rice.

Brazilian Beef Stock

✦

MAKES ABOUT 2 CUPS

Brazilian beef stock is like any other beef stock in the world and is usually prepared in the traditional time-consuming way. This is a shortcut which uses canned beef consommé and spices to approximate the taste.

One 10½-ounce can condensed beef consommé

¼ cup dry sherry

½ cup cool water

3 black peppercorns

1 bay leaf

Pinch dry thyme

Place the beef consommé, sherry, and water in a heavy saucepan. Prepare a bouquet garni by tying the herbs and spices into a piece of cheesecloth. Add the bouquet garni to the saucepan, cover, and simmer over medium heat for 15 minutes. When ready, remove the cheesecloth bag, and use.

Vatapá

This classic Bahian dish is found on street corners in Bahia where it is served as a stuffing for acarajé and on fancy dinner tables where it appears with rice as an accompanying starch. Its ingredients are familiar to all who know the lyrics of Dorival Caymmi's song "Vatapá." The recipe is basic, the trick is in adjusting the seasonings to individual tastes which is done, as the song tells us, by adding "um bocadinho mais" (a tiny bit more) until it is perfect.

1 pound stale Italian-style bread

¾ cup dried smoked shrimp (see page 35)

⅔ cup mixed roasted peanuts and cashews

¼ cup dendê (see page 39)

¼ cup peanut oil

1 cup thick coconut milk (see page 38)

¼ cup water

1 thumb-size piece fresh ginger

Salt and preserved malagueta pepper to taste

Soak the bread in water to cover for at least 1 hour. Squeeze the water from the bread and put it through a food mill. Pulverize the shrimp and nuts in a food processor. Place all the ingredients in a heavy saucepan and cook over low heat, stirring constantly, until the mixture has become a smooth paste. Add more water if necessary.

Pirão

◆

Similar to the starchy mashes of West Africa which are certainly its ancestors, a *pirão* is a starchy mixture that is prepared by adding water or other liquid to a flour. In this case coconut milk is added to rice flour, but other *pirões* can be prepared with cornmeal or cassava meal.

2 cups thin coconut milk (see page 38)

1 cup thick coconut milk (see page 38)

½ cup rice flour (see note below)

Salt to taste

Mix the coconut milks together and pour them into a medium-size saucepan, reserving a half cup. Heat the liquid over low heat. Slowly add the rice flour to the reserved coconut milk, stirring until it is completely absorbed. Gradually add the flour-and-coconut milk mixture to the heated coconut milk, stirring constantly. Continue to heat until the *pirão* becomes a stiff paste, like a cooked cereal. Pour into a buttered 4-cup mold and let cool. Serve cold with Bahian dishes.

NOTE: Rice flour can be purchased at health food stores or through the mail-order sources listed.

Angu de Milho

Corn Angu

MAKES 6 TO 8 SERVINGS

Angu is a northeastern Brazilian dish that harks back to the days of slavery. Prints by the French explorer and travel writer, Jean Baptiste Debret, show Brazilian women cooking large pots of *angu* over wood fires. A Brazilian friend confirmed that this is still done in some parts of the country and even in large cities like Rio during the pre-carnival period when the samba schools rehearse. Similar to the coocoos of the West Indies and the cornmeal mush of the southern United States, this corn *angu* is prepared simply from cornmeal and water, with the addition of a bit of butter or animal fat.

> **3 cups cold water**
>
> **2 teaspoons salt**
>
> **¾ cup cornmeal**
>
> **4 teaspoons butter**

Place half of the water in a medium-size saucepan, add the salt, and bring it to a boil over medium heat. Slowly mix the cornmeal into the remaining water. Gradually pour that mixture into the boiling water, stirring constantly. Add the butter and continue to stir constantly until the *angu* turns into a thick porridge which will hold its shape. Pour the *angu* into a well-buttered 6-cup mold. Let cool, then unmold.

Açaçá

This is a dish that comes to Brazil straight from Benin in West Africa with its name intact. *Açaçá* are balls of boiled fermented corn. They are great street snacks as their slightly tart taste is refreshing and filling. In Benin the best *açaçá* are thought to come from the small villages near Abomey, the capital of the former kingdom of Abomey. In Brazil *açaçá* are definitely a Bahian specialty. Slaves who were captured in the recurring wars between the kingdom of Abomey and its neighbor the kingdom of Oyo brought their recipes with them into their enslavement. In Brazil *açaçá* are also used to accompany stews and sauces. The mixture can also be diluted with milk and served with cinnamon and sugar as a sweet.

They are not something everyone is going to like, but then again they're not something that everyone's going to prepare because after the fermented corn has been boiled, it is placed in banana leaves which are difficult to find. For the few who are adventurous, here then, is *açaçá*.

1 cup dried white hominy corn

3 or more cups water

6 banana leaves (see page 33)

Two days before preparing the *açaçá*, soak the hominy corn overnight at room temperature in water to cover to soften it. The following day, discard the water remaining and put the hominy corn through a food mill or puree in a blender or food processor. Soak it overnight again at room temperature in water to cover, this time to allow it to ferment slightly. When ready to cook, place the water in a medium-size saucepan and bring to a boil over medium heat. Slowly add the hominy corn and 1 cup of its soaking liquid. You may have to add more water to make 1 cup. Stir until the mixture thickens into a porridge. Place two heaping serving-spoonsful onto each piece of banana leaf and roll it into a ball. Allow the balls to cool and thicken, then chill. The *acaçá* is best eaten cold.

Abacaxi Assado

Baked Pineapple

MAKES 6 TO 8 SERVINGS

This dish is simple to make and goes particularly well with roast pork and grilled chicken. The trick is to remember that the pineapple must be whole or halved. If it is cut into pieces, it will become dry. For this reason, it is a dish that is eaten with the hands as diners must bite the heated inside of the pineapple from the rind.

1 pineapple

Cut the top off of the pineapple and place it in a preheated 350°F oven for 45 minutes. Remove, cut into 8 sections and then into serving-size pieces as though making pineapple boats for dessert. Serve warm.

CARNES E FRANGOS

Meat and Poultry

BRAZIL IS THE LAND of meat and potatoes, where main dishes are king. The most typical of the main dishes, and indeed Brazil's national dish, is *feijoada:* black beans, pork and smoked meats, and various condiments. The best way to eat a *feijoada* is on a Saturday in Rio. Restaurants along the beaches serve copious *feijoada* buffets, starting around two o'clock with a few caipirinhas, followed by several *chopes* (Brazilian draft beer) with the meal. There's only one better way to while away a Saturday.

The better way? With a *feijoada* at a friend's home. If that friend is Marcelo Figuereido and the home is that of his parents in Copacabana, then the *feijoada* is the stuff that dreams are made of. Dona Alba, Marcelo's mother, had a career as a concert pianist before she became a *dona de casa* (the delicate Portuguese term for a housewife). Today she puts all of the same artistry that formerly went into playing sonatas into the creation of meals and the results are as stellar. Her husband, Don Guilherme, is a Renaissance man. Among other things he is a columnist for Rio's *O Globo* newspaper, a bon vivant, a culinary historian, and a fixture of the Rio intelligentsia.

An invitation to their home is a much-coveted event. I'm fortunate in that they are a part of my Brazilian family. On my most recent trip to Rio, they celebrated my arrival with a gathering of friends old and new. We spent the first part of the afternoon drinking caipirinihas (a leitmotif of any good Brazilian bash), nibbling on nuts, and comparing recipes.

Although scheduled to begin at one o'clock, we did not actually have lunch until about three. Marcelo joked that a good *feijoada* never begins on time. In fact, this *feijoada* was beyond good. It was superb and a lesson in the variety of cooking in Brazil. This *feijoada* was prepared as the dish is served in the northeastern province of Sergipe where Dona Alba had grown up. The main difference was that while the *feijoadas* to which I am accustomed are usually made with meat and beans, this one also included a stew of vegetables that were cooked with the beans. Cabbage, carrots, and eggplant were all a part of the dish which was so very special that Marcelo decided on the spot to baptize it *feijalba* in honor of his mother.

The company at the luncheon and the beautiful antique-and-art-filled apartment that is Don Guilherme's and Dona Alba's are far away in Rio, but when I want to recapture some of the glory of the event, I take time out (*feijalba* is not a simple dish to prepare; it takes three days!!) and begin the preparations for a *feijalba*. Invite your own literary lights and have one too. It's also a superb introduction to the traditional main dish of Brazil.

Feijalba

Feijoada Dona Alba Style

MAKES 10 TO 12 SERVINGS

**1½ pounds dried black beans, picked over
and soaked in cold water to cover overnight**

**1 pound carne seca (see page 36) cut into
2-inch pieces**

1 pound lingüiça (see page 45)

1 pound smoked pork chops

1 pound smoked back bacon, cut into 2-inch
 pieces

1 small smoked beef tongue, cut into 2-inch
 pieces

3 pig tails, well cleaned

3 pig ears, well cleaned

3 large onions, minced

3 cloves garlic, minced

¼ cup pure olive oil

Salt and freshly ground black pepper to taste

3 bay leaves

1 pound sweet cassava, (see page 30), cut
 into 2-inch pieces

1 pound sweet potatoes, peeled

1 pound small turnips

1 pound cooking pumpkin (see abóbora,
 page 28)

1 small cabbage, quartered

1 pound carots, peeled

5 firm yellow plantains (see page 32)

1 pound fresh string beans, topped, tailed,
 and tied into bunches of 10 with cotton
 string

20 kale leaves, wrapped into bunches of 5 and
 tied with cotton string

In a large stockpot, place all the meats, including the pig tails and ears that you have cleaned scrupulously, removing any hairs with tweezers and by singeing. Cover the meats with water and bring them to a boil over medium heat. Reduce the heat to low and cook for 2 hours to remove the salt and fat.

After the beans have soaked, place them and their soaking liquid in a large stockpot with cold water to cover. Allow them to cook for 1 hour over low heat, stirring occasionally so that they don't stick. Add the drained meats and continue to cook, making sure that the ingredients do not stick. Add more hot water if necessary now or any time in the cooking process; it is important to be sure that the beans always have enough liquid. As the meats cook and become fork tender, remove them from the pot. When the beans and meats are cooked, remove the stockpot from the heat, cover, and allow to remain on the stove overnight. Cover the meats with plastic wrap and refrigerate.

The following day, uncover the pot and skim off the fat with a slotted spoon. Reheat the beans over low heat. While the beans are heating, brown the onions and garlic in a large, heavy skillet over low heat in the olive oil. Season with salt and black pepper. When the beans are warmed, add 2 soupspoons of the beans and their liquid to the skillet, mash them with the back of the spoon and mix well. Then, add the mashed bean-and-onion mixture to the pot of beans along with the bay leaves, stirring well to make sure that it is thoroughly mixed.

Add the vegetables to the stockpot, in the order in which they are listed (the ones that take longest to cook will be at the bottom of the pot). The plantains are cooked in their skins. Cover the pot, adjust the heat to medium-low and cook, paying attention so that the beans do not burn or stick. (Add more hot water if necessary.) Remove the vegetables as they become fork tender and place them on a platter, and keep them warm in a low oven. When all are cooked, return the meats to the beans and let warm through. To serve, place the meats on one large platter, the vegetables on another, and the beans on a third.

Feijalba is accompanied by several side dishes. Arrange them, as my friend Marcelo says, "with as much visual caprice as possible." The full *feijalba* table includes *Molho Apimentado* (page 92), *Farofa* (page 104), White Rice (page 31), *Pimenta Malagueta* (page 88), and orange segments that have been skinned and seeded. A true *feijalba* should begin with a caipirinha (page 244) and be accompanied by beer (Brazilian if possible). Finally, as any Brazilian knows, no one should plan to do any work after a *feijalba*.

Feijoada

Smoked Meat and Black Bean Stew

MAKES 10 SERVINGS

This is the national dish of Brazil. There are as many ways to prepare *feijoada* as there are regions in Brazil and cooks in each region. I have had *feijoadas* ranging from the superrich *feijalba* prepared in the manner of Sergipe (see the preceding recipe) to a humble dish of meat-flavored beans thickened with abundant cassava meal, to a ritual *feijoada* prepared for the Yoruba god of iron and metal, Ogun, in a *terreiro* in Bahia. Each was different, yet, like variations on a theme, each had the central thread of meat, black beans, and accompaniments. This *feijoada* is a relatively simple one, as *feijoadas* go. It is designed to approximate the *feijoadas* served in beachside restaurants in Rio de Janeiro.

Saturday is traditionally *feijoada* day in Rio because after eating a *feijoada*, going back to work is unthinkable. On that day, Cariocas head for the beach in the morning and then when hungry cross the street in beach coverups to claim a seat at their favorite restaurant. There they start with a caipirinha (see page 244) and share news with friends while munching on the various *feijoada* ingredients for hours on end.

Transplanted Brazilians cannot bring their wonderful beaches with them. However, they have managed to bring their Saturday *feijoada* rituals. In Paris they gather at Chez Guy in the Latin Quarter to share gossip, drink beer, and dance and sing to samba music from a live band. In New York one of the gathering places is Via Brasil in the block of 46th Street known as Little Brazil. Wherever it is served, a *feijoada* is a feast for friends. It is a dish that cannot be made for a few and one that must be eaten with love and laughter. So if you can't have the beach at Ipanema, you can at least get together with your friends, put some Maria Bethania, Gal Costa, Gilberto Gil, and Milton Nacimento on the CD player, break out the caipirinhas and Brazilian beer, and enjoy a Brazilian afternoon.

1 pound pork shoulder

1 pound corned spareribs, if available

1 pound or more carne seca (see page 36)

½ pound chouriço (see page 37)

1 pound smoked pork shoulder

1 pound lean bacon, in one piece, rind removed

1 pound lean beef chuck, in one piece

4 cups dried black beans, picked over, soaked overnight in water to cover, and drained

2 medium-size onions, minced

2 cloves garlic, minced

1 stalk celery, minced

1 bouquet garni prepared from 3 bay leaves, 3 sprigs of fresh parsley, and 1 teaspoon dried thyme

Salt and freshly ground black pepper to taste

3½ quarts water

The evening before, rinse the salted meats in cold water and leave them to soak overnight. The next morning, change the water and allow them to continue soaking until you are ready to cook. Place all of the ingredients in a large heavy pot and bring slowly to a boil over medium heat, then reduce the heat to low and simmer for 2 hours. Remove each piece of meat when it is fork tender, starting with the beef and ending with the smoked meats. Continue to cook the beans for an additional 30 minutes, or until the liquid has become thick and creamy. Meanwhile, remove the meat from the bones and cube or slice what you can. When the beans are done, place them in a large, heavy saucepan, add the meats, and cook over low heat for 10 minutes. Remove from the heat and serve hot.

A *feijoada* is a groaning board banquet in itself. The meats can be heaped on one platter, beans put in a clay pot, and white rice in another serving dish. The garnishes must include peeled orange segments, *Farofa* (see page 104), *Couve a Mineira* (see page 142), *Molho de Pimenta e Limão* (see page 93), and *Molho Apimentado* (see page 92). Don't forget the Brazilian music for atmosphere!

Picadinho

Brazilian Minced Meat

MAKES 6 SERVINGS

This dish, whose name means "little minced meat" in Portuguese, is a Brazilian favorite. In Rio it is a favorite with hostesses because it is simple to make and yet can be presented even at a fairly formal meal. It is traditionally served with white rice. It can be made even more spicy with the addition of more malagueta pepper. You can also prepare the *picadinho* with leftover beef. If so, reduce the cooking time accordingly.

> **4 strips streaky bacon, diced**
>
> **2 pounds rump steak, cut into ½-inch cubes**
>
> **1 large onion, chopped**
>
> **2 large ripe tomatoes, peeled, seeded, and coarsely chopped**
>
> **3 preserved malagueta peppers, minced (see page 88)**
>
> **Salt and freshly ground black pepper to taste**
>
> **½ cup water**

Place the bacon in a large, heavy skillet and cook it over medium heat until crisp. Leaving the bacon bits in the skillet, add the steak, onion, tomatoes, peppers, salt, and pepper and cook, stirring, until the meat is well browned. Add the water, cover, and simmer over low heat until the meat has reached the desired doneness and the liquid becomes a thick sauce, about 10 minutes. Serve hot.

Quiabada

Beef and Okra Bahian Style

MAKES 4 SERVINGS

This dish from northeastern Brazil gets its name from one of its main ingredients, okra, which is *quiabo* in Portuguese. The okra is also a hint of the dish's African heritage. Indeed, it is similar in ingredients, if not in taste, to some of the gumbos of New Orleans.

> 2 tablespoons pure olive oil
>
> 1 large onion, minced
>
> 1 clove garlic, minced
>
> 1 pound boneless shell steak, cut into 1-inch cubes
>
> 2 medium-size ripe tomatoes, peeled, seeded, and coarsely chopped
>
> Salt and freshly ground black pepper to taste
>
> 2 preserved malagueta peppers, minced, or to taste (see page 88)
>
> 1 pound small unblemished fresh okra pods, topped, tailed, and sliced into rounds

Heat the oil in a large, heavy skillet over medium heat. Add the onion and garlic and cook, stirring, until they are soft. Add the meat and cook, stirring occasionally to cook all sides, until it is browned. Add the tomatoes and seasonings. Cover, reduce the heat to low, and cook until the meat is cooked to the desired doneness and there is a reddish sauce, 7 to 10 minutes. Meanwhile, blanch the okra by placing it in a saucepan of boiling salted water and cooking it for 3 to 5 minutes. Drain the okra and add it to the meat. Cook for an additional 5 minutes. Serve hot with *Angu* (see page 162) or white rice.

Churrasco

Gaucho Style Brazilian Barbecue

MAKES 4 SERVINGS

Most folks think only of Argentina when they think of pampas. However, Brazil, too, has its grasslands and its cowboys who are also called gauchos. They have perfected their own methods of barbecuing beef. Their techniques have become the basis for some of the most popular restaurants in large cities like Rio, São Paulo, and even Salvador. Called *churrascarias,* they specialize in grilled meats. In some, like Marius' in Rio de Janeiro, they serve *rodízio* style, with waiters circulating with heavy swords of meat from which individual diners select the cuts they wish. A small amount is served at the diner's request, but the dance of the waiters and the swords is unceasing and diners can eat virtually as much as they want. The taste of the restaurants can be approximated at home with an outdoor grill. However, for true *churrasco,* you need an open fire, the vast pampas, and a gaucho.

Four 1½-inch-thick shell steaks

¾ cup fresh lime juice

⅓ cup dry red wine

1 small onion, minced

2 cloves garlic, minced

2 teaspoons dried oregano

1 bay leaf

1 teaspoon freshly ground black pepper

Salt to taste

Leave the steaks in a marinade prepared with the remaining ingredients for at least overnight (longer if possible). When ready to barbecue, remove them from the marinade, pat dry with paper towels, and grill on both sides until the desired level of doneness. You can prepare the *churrasco* indoors in the broiler, but you will not have the same taste. Serve the steaks with white rice and *Molho Campanha* (see page 91).

Stroganoff

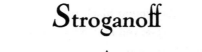

MAKES 4 SERVINGS

This would certainly seem to be a dish that has found its way into the wrong cookbook. In fact, stroganoff is one of Brazil's most popular dishes. Brought by immigrants from Eastern Europe in the late nineteenth and early twentieth centuries, the dish has grown in popularity over the years. Today it is so popular that even Brazilian restaurants outside of Brazil serve it for homesick natives. Brazilian stroganoff is different from the classic one in many ways. The most important is that it is not served over noodles, but over white rice.

2 tablespoons salted butter

1 large onion, minced

1 clove garlic, minced

½ pound white cultivated mushrooms,
   quartered

1½ pounds leftover roast beef, cut into strips
   (see note below)

2 tablespoons cognac

1 teaspoon Worcestershire sauce

Salt, freshly ground black pepper, and
   minced preserved malagueta pepper (see
   page 88) to taste

¼ cup sour cream

Melt the butter in a large, heavy skillet over medium heat. Add the onion and garlic and cook, stirring, until browned. Add the remaining ingredients and cook, stirring occasionally to make sure that none of the ingredients stick to the pan, for 5 minutes. Serve immediately with white rice.

NOTE: If you don't have leftover roast beef, you can substitute fresh shell steak cut into strips, but you must then lengthen the cooking time about 10 minutes or so, depending on the desired degree of doneness.

Shabu Shabu

Japanese Boiled Dinner

MAKES 4 SERVINGS

São Paulo in southern Brazil boasts the largest Japanese population outside of Japan. On my first trip there, one of the things that I insisted on doing with my friend Nair was have a Japanese dinner. She took me to her favorite restaurant which was located on a small side street not far from my hotel. We entered and found that the restaurant had several sections. One specialized in tempura and served such Brazilian-influenced dishes as a tempura which had alongside the traditional shrimp and vegetables, batter-fried pieces of sweet cassava. The second room featured griddle tables where chefs could cook as people watched. In the third there was a sushi bar. We had my favorite dish, *shabu shabu,* which was cooked at the table in a heavy iron pot. Here is the recipe, a testimony to all the Japanese who traveled to Brazil and made it their home.

> 2 pieces tofu, cut into 1-inch squares
>
> 4 scallions, both green and white parts, cut into diagonal pieces
>
> 8 large white cultivated mushrooms, sliced
>
> 2 large carrots, thinly sliced
>
> 1 piece konbu (see note below)
>
> 4 cups water
>
> ½ pound fresh spinach, washed thoroughly and stems removed
>
> ¼ bok choy, cut into pieces (see note on next page)
>
> 1 pound filet mignon, cut into thin slices (see note on next page)

Shabu shabu is prepared at the table, so no advance cooking is involved. Begin by preparing the tofu and vegetables and arranging them on a serving plate. Then place a heavy iron pot on a hot plate or portable gas burner. Put the piece of konbu in the pot, add the water, cover the pot, and allow the water to come to a boil. When the water is boiling, uncover the pot, remove the konbu, and begin to cook. Diners select the pieces that they want and cook them to taste in the pot. When the pieces are ready, they are dipped in the sauce (recipe follows), and eaten with white rice.

NOTE: Thinly sliced beef for *shabu shabu* is available at Japanese stores. If slicing the meat at home, partially freeze the meat first, then slice against the grain.

Konbu, a seaweed, is available in Japanese stores. Bok choy, or Chinese cabbage, can be found in Asian food markets.

Ponzu

Dipping Sauce for Shabu Shabu

MAKES ¾ CUP

¼ cup soy sauce

¼ cup fresh lemon juice

¼ cup water

Mix the ingredients together in a bowl and place a bit in a small bowl for each diner. *Ponzu* is traditionally served with a small dish of grated daikon radish and minced scallion. Diners add the amount they prefer to their own bowl.

Costeletas de Porco

Pork Chops

MAKES 4 SERVINGS

These pan-fried pork chops are delicious when served by themselves. When they are served with *Tutu a Mineira* (see page 144) and *Couve a Mineira* (page 142), the entire dish is known as *Tutu a Mineira* and is a specialty of the Minas Gerais region of Brazil.

Eight ½-inch thick pork chops

¼ cup fresh lemon juice

1 clove garlic, chopped

Salt, freshly ground black pepper, and minced habanero chile (see page 88) to taste

1 tablespoon pure olive oil

Wash the pork chops, trim off any excess fat, and pat them dry with paper towels. Place the pork chops in a marinade prepared from the lemon juice, garlic, and seasonings and allow to stand in the refrigerator for at least an hour. Heat the olive oil in a heavy skillet over medium-high heat. Remove the chops from the marinade, pat dry, and place them in the skillet (use two skillets if necessary to avoid crowding them). Pan fry for 10 to 15 minutes, turning frequently. Serve hot.

Paçoca de Carne Seca

Paçoca of Dried Meat

MAKES 4 TO 6 SERVINGS

This dish which is typical of the region of Pernambuco in Brazil's northeast can only be prepared if you can find the typical Brazilian meat *carne seca*. This meat is the central ingredient in many a *feijoada*. As one Brazilian friend puts it, "It's tough, but delicious." Here, the *carne seca* is the basis for a paste that is prepared with cassava meal. Traditionally, *paçoca* is prepared in a large wooden mortar with a pestle, but this version uses a food processor with almost the same result.

> 1 pound carne seca (see page 36)
>
> ½ pound fatty bacon, diced
>
> 4 medium-size onions, chopped
>
> 12 black peppercorns
>
> 1 pound cassava meal (see page 31)

Soak the *carne seca* in water to cover for five hours in the refrigerator, changing the water once. When the *carne seca* is ready, cut it into small pieces and fry them with the bacon until crisp in a large, heavy skillet over medium-high heat. Remove the meat with a slotted spoon, drain on paper towels, and cook the onions in the remaining fat over medium heat, stirring, until they are golden. Then place the meat, onions, and peppercorns in a food processor and pulse them slowly. Gradually add the cassava meal, a bit at a time, until you have a smooth, thick paste. If the paste becomes too thick, add a small amount of water. The *paçoca* is served warm with white rice.

Frango Grelhado

Grilled Chicken

At my favorite New York Brazilian restaurant, one of the dishes that I order frequently is a simple grilled chicken. It comes served with white rice (see page 31) and black beans (page 41) and I always ask for a large bowl of the *Molho Apimentado* (page 92) that they use to go with grilled steak. The result is a simple, delicious combination.

> **One 3- to 4-pound roasting chicken,**
> **quartered**
>
> **2 tablespoons pure olive oil**
>
> **Salt and freshly ground black pepper to taste**

Place the chicken in a roasting pan and coat it with the olive oil, salt, and pepper. Place it under a preheated broiler or place the pieces on a hot grill and cook them for 10 to 15 minutes on each side, or until cooked through (no red joints please!). Remove and serve hot with *Molho Apimentado* (page 92).

Ximxim de Galinha

*Chicken with Peanuts and Cashews
Bahian Style*

MAKES 4 TO 6 SERVINGS

This is another classic dish from the Bahian culinary repertoire. The yellow-tinged chicken-and-peanut stew speaks immediately of its West African origin, with its use of palm oil (*dendê*). Africa is also seen in the use of dried smoked shrimp and ground cashews and peanuts. I first tasted this dish at a folkloric restaurant in Bahia, located in an old plantation house, the Solar de Unhão. Later I would discover that *ximxim* is also one of the dishes prepared in the Candomblé religion and served to the goddess of love and wealth, Oxum. It is fitting that this is one of Oxum's dishes because the dish itself is a rich one and when finished with palm oil, it is also Oxum's favorite color, golden yellow.

> One 3- to 4-pound chicken, cut into serving
>   pieces
>
> Juice of 2 lemons
>
> Salt and freshly ground black pepper to taste
>
> ¼ pound dried smoked shrimp, shelled (see
>   page 35)
>
> 1 large onion, quartered
>
> 2 medium-size ripe tomatoes, peeled, seeded,
>   and coarsely chopped
>
> 2 tablespoons pure olive oil
>
> 1 clove garlic, minced
>
> ¾ cup water
>
> 1 pound jumbo shrimp

4 preserved malagueta peppers or to taste
   (see page 88)

2 tablespoons ground roasted cashew nuts

1 tablespoon ground roasted peanuts

½ teaspoon minced fresh ginger

3 tablespoons dendê (see page 39)

Marinate the chicken pieces in the lemon juice, salt, and pepper for half an hour. Grind the dried shrimp in a food processor with the onion and tomatoes into a thick paste. In a large saucepan, heat the oil over medium heat. Add the garlic and cook, stirring, until browned. Add the onion, tomato, and shrimp paste and the drained chicken pieces. Brown the chicken pieces on all sides, then add ¼ cup of the water bit by bit, cover the pot, reduce the heat to low, and cook for 35 to 40 minutes, or until the chicken is almost cooked. Be sure that the mixture does not boil and stir occasionally so that the chicken pieces do not stick to the pan. Add the jumbo shrimp, malagueta peppers, and ground nuts. Check the seasonings. Add the ginger and remaining water and finish cooking by bringing the mixture to a boil. When ready to serve, drizzle the *dendê* over the *ximxim* and cook for a few more minutes. Serve hot with white rice and *Farofa de Dendê* (see page 105).

Galinha Assado com Abacaxi

Pineapple Chicken

MAKES 4 SERVINGS

This is a way with pineapple that was taught to me by my friend Erminha. It's simple to make and delicious. The pineapple-and-onion stuffing is a great accompaniment to the dish and the chicken comes out of the oven juicy and with a faint taste of pineapple.

One 3- to 4-pound roasting chicken

3 cups fresh pineapple chunks, drained and liquid reserved

1 medium-size onion, coarsely chopped

Salt and freshly ground black pepper to taste

4 tablespoons (½ stick) butter

Preheat the oven to 400°F. Clean the chicken inside and out and place it in a roasting pan. Mix the pineapple chunks with the onion, and season. Place the mixture into the cavity of the chicken. Cut 1 tablespoon of the butter into pieces, lift the breast skin of the chicken and insert the pieces. Melt the rest of the butter and mix it together with the reserved juice from the pineapple pieces. Pour it over the chicken, then place the chicken in the oven and roast for 1 hour, basting it occasionally. After an hour, reset the oven to 450°F and continue to cook the chicken for 15 minutes. Remove from the oven, let rest 5 minutes, then slice and serve with the pineapple-onion mixture as a side dish.

Coxas Apimentadas

Spicy Thighs

MAKES 4 SERVINGS

Even though the name of this dish seems to be better suited to a soft porn movie, the dish is one that simply puts together broiled chicken thighs and the spicy liquid that is found in the ever handy bottles of Brazil's *pimenta malagueta*. If you cannot find *pimenta malagueta* (see page 00), you can substitute Tabasco sauce or another hot sauce, but the taste will be slightly different.

8 chicken thighs

1 tablespoon liquid from a bottle of malagueta peppers, or to taste

Salt and freshly ground black pepper to taste

Wash the chicken thighs and place them in a broiling pan. Brush the malagueta liquid over them. Place the thighs under a preheated broiler for about 10 minutes on each side, or until well done. Remove and serve with *Molho Campanha* (see page 91) or, if you really like it spicy, *Molho Apimentado* (see page 92) or *Molho Rita* (page 98).

Salada de Galinha e Abacaxi

Chicken and Pineapple Salad

MAKES 4 SERVINGS

Even in a country of meateaters, warm climates will produce one or two salads. This is particularly true with modern cooks in today's Brazil. Diet consciousness has created a segment of the population which looks for salad ideas. One of them, my friend Nair, created this interesting chicken salad using smoked chicken, raisins, pineapple, Brazil nuts, the ingredients that she had in the refrigerator at the time.

> **1 bunch watercress**
>
> **1 small head Boston lettuce, separated into leaves**
>
> **4 cups diced smoked chicken**
>
> **1 cup fresh pineapple chunks**
>
> **½ cup golden raisins**
>
> **¼ cup chopped Brazil nuts**
>
> **¼ cup Molho para Salada (see page 100)**
>
> **2 tablespoons fresh pineapple juice**

Arrange the watercress and lettuce on a medium-size platter. Mix the chicken, pineapple, and raisins together in a medium-size bowl and place the mixture on top of the greens. Cover the platter with plastic wrap and place it in the refrigerator for one hour. When ready to serve, sprinkle the Brazil nuts on top. Serve with *molho para salada* to which you have added the fresh pineapple juice.

PEIXES E
FRUTOS DO MAR

Fish and Seafood

BRAZIL HAS over 4,300 miles of coastline. It is only natural, then, that the bounty of the ocean should play such a large role on the nation's table. Local market stands, whether in Rio or in Bahia in Belém or in São Paulo, are laden with fish and shellfish still pearled with drops of ocean water. In the country's interior, the Amazon and its tributaries contribute such fish as the enormous pirarucú which was my first taste of the sea in Brazil. The tasty morsels of the firm white-fleshed fish were served up during a party that was held in a cove formed by one of the tributaries of the Amazon. The slightly sweetish taste of the fish will always be connected in my mind with the guitarist singing Bahian songs and the coolness of the water on that particular day.

That party was only the beginning of my love for Brazilian fish and seafood dishes. I've since then sampled *moquecas* and *ensopados* in Bahia. One night working with some friends who were preparing to cook *moquecas* for a large crowd, I learned that the difference between the two is simply the palm oil that is added to the *moquecas*. I've watched fishermen in Fortaleza haul in their nets and head out to the ocean in frail balsa wood rafts called *jangadas*. Later, in that city's seaside restaurants, I've savored fried fish that I'd seen the fishermen haul in. I've attended lobster parties in Bahia where the spiny lobsters came to the table freshly grilled and yet still tangy with the sea's salt. In the morning in Rio, I've marveled at the variety of fish and seafood available in local markets: sardines, flounder, snapper, octopus, shrimp in all sizes, spiny lobster, and more. In the evening, I've driven with friends out beyond the beaches to waterfront restaurants and savored the same delights prepared in myriad ways at one of the city's seafood buffet restaurants. I've even sampled Brazilian-style tekkamaki or tuna roll and snacked on sushi in São Paulo.

The country's taste for fish and seafood is as voracious as my own. And yet, no matter what the dish sampled, when the sea and its bounty are mentioned, my thoughts always first turn to that simple skewer of pirarucú I had on my first day in Brazil in the cool waters of the secluded Amazon cove.

Peixe Frita Fortaleza

Fried Fish Fortaleza

MAKES 4 SERVINGS

Fortaleza is a city on Brazil's northern coast. Known for its beaches and wonderful linens, Fortaleza has become a mecca for Brazilians who want to get away from things for a few days. Those who head to the city visit the museum which is located in the former city jail and has an extraordinary collection of carved wooden *ex votos* from nearby towns, shop in the stalls displaying beautifully embroidered baby clothing and handmade sheets, and stroll along the streets facing the sea, watching the fishermen set out in their frail-looking wooden rafts called *jangadas*. Finally, they are sure to stop at one of the seaside restaurants and enjoy some of the best fish in Brazil, prepared simply and served with only wedges of lemon as garnish.

2 pounds fresh fish fillets (flounder, scrod, or
  other firm white fish)

¼ cup fresh lemon juice

Salt and freshly ground black pepper to taste

Vegetable oil for frying

¼ cup milk

¼ cup flour

2 tablespoons cassava meal (see page 31)

Lemon wedges for garnish

Place the fish fillets in a bowl, cover them with the lemon juice, salt, and pepper and let marinate for 1 hour. Heat 2 inches of oil over medium-high heat to 350°F in a large, heavy skillet or deep fryer. Remove the fillets from the lemon juice and pat them lightly with paper towels. Dip them into the milk and then into a mixture of the flour and cassava meal. Fry them in the oil for about 2 minutes on each side, or until golden brown. Drain the fillets on paper towels and serve hot garnished with lemon wedges.

Sardinhas Grelhadas

Grilled Sardines

MAKES 6 SERVINGS

In the markets in Rio, it is possible to see small flattened-out sardines. When I first asked about them, a friend explained that they had been prepared for grilling. Grilled sardines can be found on many menus and can also be prepared easily at home. You do not have to remove the central bone and flatten them out; they're just fine cooked whole (or with the heads removed for the squeamish). Be sure to have plenty of lemon juice. If you're cooking them on an outdoor grill, use a grill basket and rub a bit of olive oil on the fish to prevent them from sticking to it.

> **18 medium-size fresh sardines (see page 51)**
>
> **¼ cup fresh lemon juice**
>
> **Salt and freshly ground black pepper to taste**
>
> **Lemon wedges for garnish**

Wash the sardines and rub them with the lemon juice and seasonings. Place them in the grill basket and cook them for about 3 to 5 minutes on each side, or until done. If you're broiling, rub the sardines with olive oil, then place them on a grilling rack that will fit inside of the pan in your broiler. Cook them as for grilled sardines. Serve hot with the lemon wedges.

Peixe Vermelho Escaldado

Poached Red Snapper Nair

MAKES 4 SERVINGS

My friend Nair de Carvalho and I have many things in common. We are both fanatics about Bahia and visit the city as often as possible. We are both admirers of authors Jorge Amado and Antonio Olinto. (Nair is their friend. She introduced me to Amado on one of my early trips to Bahia for which I am eternally grateful.) And finally, we both love to cook. Nair and I both pride ourselves on being able to go into a kitchen and prepare something from simply the ingredients that are there. On a recent trip to Brazil, Nair told of a party at a friend's house which went on until the wee hours with no food. Finally tired of the enforced and unplanned fast, Nair went into the kitchen and found a red snapper, coriander, garlic, lemons, and three kiwis. Voilà Poached Red Snapper Nair! What happened to the kiwis? They became the kiwi mayonnaise that is served with the dish (see pages 102, 103).

1 clove garlic, minced

Juice of 3 lemons

1 sprig fresh coriander (cilantro)

Salt to taste

One 2-pound whole red snapper

6 cups water

Prepare a marinade from the garlic, lemon juice, coriander, and salt and place the fish in it for 1 hour.

Pour the water in a large, heavy pot and bring it to a boil over medium-high heat. Place the fish in the liquid and allow it to come back to the boil. Remove the fish, drain on paper towels, and place it in the refrigerator to chill. The poached snapper is served cold with kiwi mayonnaise.

Mariscada

Brazilian Fish Stew

MAKES 8 TO 10 SERVINGS

Brazil's many miles of coastline mean that fish plays a major role in the country's diet. The sea's bounty is prepared in a variety of ways, from fried simply to stewed. Influences range from those of Africa that appear in the dishes of Bahia and the northeast to those of Portugal and the Mediterranean region which are prevalent in the south. This fish stew is one of the latter, where all you need is a bit of racasse—a Mediterranean fish necessary for true bouillabaisse—to feel that the winds are blowing from the Mediterranean and not from the Atlantic.

12 clams

1 pound mussels

2 tablespoons pure olive oil

1 large onion, diced

2 large ripe tomatoes, peeled, seeded, and coarsely chopped

2 cloves garlic, minced

1 sprig fresh coriander (cilantro), minced

Salt and freshly ground black pepper to taste

Cayenne pepper to taste

Pinch of saffron threads

4 pounds fresh codfish fillets, cut into serving-size pieces

1 pound jumbo shrimp, peeled and deveined

½ pound fresh crabmeat, picked over for
    cartilage

Clean the clams by scrubbing them thoroughly with a wire brush, removing any beard or barnacles. Then place them in a large pot with 1 gallon of water or enough to cover, and ⅓ cup salt. Allow the clams to remain for 20 minutes during which time they will expel the sand inside. Continue this process, changing the water at least two more times. The mussels are cleaned in a similar manner, but you must leave them in the water for at least 2 hours. Throw away any clams or mussels that float or are not tightly closed.

Heat the olive oil in the bottom of a large, heavy saucepan over medium heat. Add the onion, tomatoes, garlic, coriander, salt, peppers, and saffron and cook, stirring, until the onions have softened, but are not brown. Add the fish and shellfish to the onion mixture. Cover with water and bring to a boil. Reduce the heat to low and simmer for 10 minutes, or until the shellfish open. Discard any clams or mussels that do not open. Serve hot.

Moqueca de Peixe

Bahian Style Fish Stew

MAKES 4 SERVINGS

A *moqueca* is a fish stew from Bahia. You can tell that it is from Bahia because it includes two of the three ingredients that Brazil's culinary historians laughingly call the Holy Trinity of Bahian cooking: coconut milk and *dendê* (palm oil). The third, malagueta pepper, is occasionally added at the table by those with a taste for the piquant. There are several ways to prepare a *moqueca*. This is the first way that I learned.

3 sprigs fresh coriander (cilantro)

1 medium-size ripe tomato, quartered

½ medium-size green bell pepper, seeded

1 medium-size onion, quartered

Salt and freshly ground black pepper to taste

2 pounds fish fillets (cod, scrod, haddock, or other white, firm-fleshed fish)

1 tablespoon fresh lemon juice

½ cup thin coconut milk (see page 38)

2 tablespoons dendê (see page 39)

2 tablespoons peanut oil

Chop the coriander, tomato, pepper, and onion in a food processor until you have a coarse paste. Then place the mixture in a large, heavy skillet over low heat. Add the salt and pepper and cook for 15 minutes. Add the fish fillets to the mixture and continue cooking for an additional 5 to 7 minutes. Add the remaining ingredients, stir and allow to simmer for 5 minutes. Serve the *moqueca* hot with white rice and *Farofa Amarela* (see page 107).

Bobó de Camarão

Shrimp and Cassava Bahian Style

Bobó de Camarão is a classic dish from the northeastern Brazilian state of Bahia. Even if the dish's name had not retained its African sonorities, you'd know this because the dish has in it two of the hallmarks of Bahian cooking, palm oil, called *dendê* in Brazil, and coconut milk, mixed with such New World ingredients as sweet cassava and tomatoes. The result is delicious. This dish is the favorite of my friend who arranged my first trip to Brazil, Marlene Schwartz, who is Brazilian despite her European-sounding name.

> 1 pound sweet cassava (see page 30), peeled and quartered
>
> 2 tablespoons pure olive oil
>
> 1 large onion, minced
>
> 3 large ripe tomatoes, peeled, seeded, and coarsely chopped
>
> 2 pounds jumbo shrimp, peeled and deveined
>
> 2 tablespoons minced fresh coriander (cilantro)
>
> Salt and freshly ground black pepper to taste
>
> ½ cup thin coconut milk (see page 38)
>
> 2 tablespoons dendê (see page 39)

Cook the cassava in water to cover in a heavy saucepan over medium-high heat for 30 minutes, until fork tender. When done, puree the cassava in a blender or food processor, adding as much as ¾ cup of water to get a smooth paste. Set aside. Meanwhile, heat the oil in a large, heavy saucepan over medium heat. Add the onion and cook, stirring, until golden brown. Add the tomatoes and cook another 5 minutes. Add the shrimp, coriander, and seasonings, reduce the heat to low, cover, and cook 5 minutes, or until the shrimp are cooked through. Finally, stir in the pureed cassava, coconut milk, and *dendê*, stirring well to thoroughly mix. Bring the *bobó* back to a boil, remove from the heat, and serve hot with white rice.

Caruru

MAKES 6 SERVINGS

This is a dish that comes to Brazil's northeast from West Africa, Yorubaland to be exact. The Yoruba have the highest incidence of twin birth in the world and the twins there are celebrated with carved figures called *ibejis*, in music, in song, in legend, and, yes, in food. This veneration of twins has been continued in Brazil where families with twins honor them annually with a feast of *caruru* on the feast day of the twin Roman Catholic saints, Cosme and Damian. A few years ago, when I presented a dish of *caruru* on "Good Morning America," I brought along not only the yellow-hued shrimp-filled dish, but also a pair of Yoruba twin figures from my African art collection. They were the hit of the show.

2 pounds small unblemished fresh okra,
topped, tailed, and cut into small pieces

Juice of 2 lemons

2 tablespoons dendê (see page 39)

1 medium-size onion, minced

1 clove garlic, minced

4 sprigs fresh coriander (cilantro), minced

3 tablespoons ground dried smoked shrimp
(see page 35)

1 pound jumbo shrimp, peeled and deveined

⅓ cup roasted peanuts

Salt and freshly ground black pepper to taste

¾ cup water

Liquid from bottle of malagueta pepper to
taste (see page 88)

12 cooked jumbo shrimp for garnish (see
page 34)

Soak the okra in the lemon juice to which a pinch of salt has been
added. In a large, heavy skillet, heat the *dendê* over medium heat. Add
the onion, garlic, and coriander and cook, stirring, until browned. In
a food processor or blender, grind the smoked and fresh shrimp and
peanuts. Add these, along with the okra, salt, and pepper to the
contents of the skillet. Pour in the water and cook the *caruru* over low
heat for 30 minutes, stirring occasionally. When ready, add a few
drops of malagueta pepper liquid. Serve garnished with the cooked
shrimp along with white rice and *Farofa Amarela* (see page 107).

Espetinhos de Camarão

Shrimp Skewers

MAKES 4 SERVINGS

Shrimp are a standby in many coastal Brazilian households where they are served in a multitude of guises. In this recipe, they are simply grilled and served with white rice. Occasionally, if larger shrimp are used, they are split, stuffed with cassava meal, and placed two to a skewer. In that case, with traditional Brazilian culinary humor, they are called *Camarões Casadinhos*, or married prawns.

2 pounds jumbo shrimp, peeled and deveined

½ cup fresh lemon juice

1 clove garlic, minced

1 small onion, minced

1 bay leaf

Salt and freshly ground black pepper to taste

Place the shrimp in a marinade prepared with the remaining ingredients. Cover with plastic wrap and allow to sit refrigerated for at least 2 hours. Soak the skewers in water for 15 minutes so that they will not burn. Remove the shrimp from the marinade and place them on small wooden skewers. Heat the grill to cooking temperature and place the shrimp on the grill. Cook for about 2 to 3 minutes on each side, or until pink and nicely browned. Serve hot.

Camarões a Paulista

São Paulo Style Shrimp

MAKES 4 SERVINGS

Shellfish abound in the waters off Brazil's coast and the natives of Rio and São Paulo make it their business to enjoy them as often as possible. In sophisticated São Paulo, residents pride themselves on having some of the best restaurants in the country. However, when Paulists eat at home, they frequently have this shrimp dish that bears their name.

> 16 jumbo shrimp or 4 per person, add more
>   to taste, peeled and deveined
>
> Juice of 5 limes
>
> 1 clove garlic, minced
>
> 1 small onion, minced
>
> 2 sprigs fresh coriander (cilantro), coarsely
>   chopped
>
> Salt and freshly ground black pepper to taste
>
> Fresh coriander sprigs and lime halves for
>   garnish

Place the shrimp in a glass bowl with a marinade made from the lime juice, garlic, onion, chopped coriander, salt, and pepper. Allow them to marinate for two hours. Remove them from the marinade, drain, and place on skewers, four to a skewer. Place them on aluminum foil under a preheated broiler and grill for 2 to 3 minutes on each side, or until done. Serve garnished with sprigs of coriander and lime halves.

Moqueca de Camarão

Bahian Style Shrimp Stew

Many different types of seafoods (see page 197) can be made into *moquecas*. There are even chicken *moquecas* and egg *moquecas* (see page 157). This is another way of making them using fresh large shrimp.

⅓ cup pure olive oil

2 medium-size onions, sliced

1 small green bell pepper, seeded and sliced crosswise

2 small ripe tomatoes, sliced

1 teaspoon chopped fresh coriander (cilantro)

1 clove garlic, minced

1 tablespoon tomato paste

12 cooked jumbo shrimp, peeled and deveined (see page 34)

2 tablespoons fresh lemon juice

½ cup thin coconut milk (see page 38)

¼ cup dendê (see page 39)

Heat the olive oil in a large, heavy skillet over medium-high heat. Add the onions, pepper, tomatoes, coriander, garlic, and tomato paste and cook, stirring, until the onions are translucent. Bring the sauce to a boil, then add the shrimp and lemon juice. Reduce the heat to medium and cook for 2 to 3 minutes, or until the shrimp are heated through. Then add the coconut milk and *dendê* and bring the mixture to a boil again for a minute. Check the seasonings and serve hot, over white rice.

Lagosta Grelhada

Grilled Lobster

MAKES 2 SERVINGS

The Hotel Bahia Othon boasts a poolside restaurant where one of
the specialties is grilled lobster. The lobster in Bahia is the warm
water spiny type with none of the claw meat so prized by aficionados
of the Maine version. However, they are as delicious and succulent.
They are grilled in their shells and come to the table with a hint of
two of the primal elements: the salt tang of the sea and the charred,
grilled savor of the fire. Try this with spiny lobsters if you live in a
warm area, or with lobster tails anywhere else.

> 2 large spiny lobsters or 4 lobster tails (see
> page 44)
>
> 3 limes
>
> 2 tablespoons salted butter
>
> 1 tablespoon minced fresh parsley
>
> Salt and freshly ground black pepper to taste
>
> Lemon and lime wedges for garnish
>
> Minced fresh parsley for garnish
>
> Melted butter for dipping

Heat the grill. If working with fresh lobsters, cut them in half. With
lobster tails, you will simply place them on the grill, shell side down.
Melt the butter in a small saucepan and mix with the parsley, salt,
and pepper. Drizzle the butter sauce over the lobsters. Cook for 10
to 12 minutes, or until done, turning once. Garnish with lemon and
lime wedges and parsley and serve hot with melted butter on the
side.

Ensopado de Lagosta

Lobster and Coconut Milk

———— ✦ ————

MAKES 4 SERVINGS

While *moquecas* are typical of the cooking of Bahia, many Americans are wary of *dendê*, or palm oil (see page 39 for more information) and would prefer not to eat this highly saturated oil. When I explained this to my friends in Bahia, they laughed saying, that's no problem for us. When they make a *moqueca* without the *dendê* it becomes an *ensopado*, or a stew prepared simply with coconut milk.

> **2 pounds fresh lobster meat**
>
> **1 clove garlic, sliced**
>
> **½ teaspoon salt**
>
> **1 teaspoon chopped fresh coriander (cilantro)**
>
> **Freshly ground black pepper to taste**
>
> **Juice of 2 lemons**
>
> **⅓ cup pure olive oil**
>
> **2 medium-size onions, sliced**
>
> **1 small green bell pepper, seeded and sliced**
>
> **1 large ripe tomato, peeled, seeded, and sliced**
>
> **¾ cup thin coconut milk (see page 38)**

Place the lobster meat in a large bowl with a marinade prepared with the garlic, salt, half the coriander, the black pepper, and lemon juice. Cover it with a sheet of aluminum foil or plastic wrap and let it sit for 2 hours in the refrigerator.

Heat the oil in a large, heavy skillet over medium heat. Add the onions, green pepper, tomato, and remaining coriander and cook, stirring occasionally, until the onions are translucent. Add the lobster meat and the marinade and cook another 5 to 7 minutes, or until the lobster is opaque all the way through. Add the coconut milk and bring the mixture to a boil. Cook for 2 to 3 minutes, check the seasonings, and serve hot with white rice.

Efo

MAKES 4 SERVINGS

This is one of the dishes of northeastern Brazil that arrived there directly from the Slave Coast of West Africa. The use of dried smoked shrimp, of hot malagueta peppers, and of *dendê* (palm oil) speaks of the dish's African origins, as does its way with greens, in this case, spinach.

> 2 tablespoons dried smoked shrimp, peeled if
> necessary (see page 35)
>
> 1 pound cooked shrimp, peeled (see page 34)
>
> 1 clove garlic
>
> 2 medium-size onions, quartered
>
> 4 preserved malagueta pepper (see page 88)
>
> 1 teaspoon minced fresh coriander (cilantro)
>
> 3 pounds fresh spinach, washed thoroughly,
> stems removed, and shredded
>
> 2 tablespoons pure olive oil
>
> 1 pound fresh crabmeat, picked over for
> cartilage and shredded
>
> 1 large ripe tomato, peeled, seeded, and
> coarsely chopped
>
> 1 tablespoon dendê (see page 39)
>
> Salt and freshly ground black pepper to taste

Put the smoked and cooked shrimp, garlic, onions, peppers, and coriander in a food processor or blender and grind them to a fine paste. Place the spinach over medium heat in a large, covered saucepan, using only the moisture from the washed leaves to steam it for 5 minutes. When done, add the shrimp paste to the spinach. In a medium-size, heavy skillet heat the olive oil over medium heat. Add the crabmeat and cook, stirring a few times, until browned. Add the crabmeat to the shrimp-and-spinach mixture. Stir in the tomato, *dendê*, salt, and black pepper and verify the seasoning. Continue to cook, stirring occasionally, for 2 minutes and serve with *Acaçá* (see page 163).

Frigideira de Siri

Bahian Crab Bake

MAKES 4 SERVINGS

My friend, Brazilian artist Nair de Carvalho, lives in Bahia and in São Paulo. She is a world traveler who has exhibited her sun-filled artwork around the world. When we talk about Brazilian food, she always says that the one Bahian dish that she always prepares for guests when she is not in Brazil is *Frigideira de Siri* because it is Bahian and yet does not require *dendê* (palm oil). The dish gets its name from the earthenware casserole in which it is traditionally cooked, a *frigideira*. The dish, in turn, gets its name from the main use to which it is put, frying, in Portuguese, *frigir*.

1 coconut

1 pound fresh crabmeat, picked over for
cartilage

¼ cup pure olive oil

4 large ripe tomatoes, peeled, seeded, and
coarsely chopped

2 large onions, coarsely chopped

1 clove garlic, minced

2 sprigs fresh coriander (cilantro), minced

Salt, freshly ground black pepper, and
minced preserved malagueta pepper (see
page 88) to taste

4 large eggs

Extract the coconut milk from the coconut (see page 37). Pulse half
of the crabmeat in a food processor and reserve. Heat the oil over
medium heat in a heavy skillet and cook the remaining crabmeat, the
tomatoes, onions, garlic, and coriander, stirring, until the onions are
soft, but not brown. Add the coconut milk and reserved crabmeat.
Add the seasonings and cook, covered, for 10 minutes over low heat.
Preheat the oven to 375°F. Beat the eggs and pour them into the
crabmeat mixture. Mix well and pour the *frigideira* into an ovenproof
dish. Bake for 15 minutes. Serve hot.

DOCES E BOLOS

Sweets and Desserts

YOU CAN SEE THEM on street corners in the cities of Brazil. They're decked out in the white lace garments that are the hallmarks of those who worship the African gods, or *orixás*. These garments have become for many Brazilians the traditional equivalent of chef's whites for Europeans. These garments are a silent testimony to the authenticity of the food and to the virtuosity of the cook. The women who wear them hark back to the days of slavery when many a talented slave cook was allowed to sell her wares in the street, bringing the profits home for the mistress and occasionally keeping a percentage which might someday allow her to purchase her freedom. Today they're still there, dressed in their foamy froth of lace. Their necks are ladened with ropes of multicolored glass beads which signal the *orixá* of their devotion. Their heads are wrapped in pristine white turbans and their arms are heavy with gold and silver bracelets. They are called *Baianas de tabuleiro* (Bahian ladies with trays).

Dorival Caymmi, the noted Bahian songwriter, has a song about the trays of the Bahian women. In the lyrics he talks of all of their savory goodies. However, *Baianas* are also noted throughout Brazil for the variety and the delicacy of their sweets and desserts. Other songs sing of the *quindins* of yaya (Mother-in-law's coconut cakes), and of other delicacies. Desserts include candies, compotes, candied tropical fruits, stewed tropical fruits, fruit salads and ice creams, nut confections, and the entire range of what can be done with coconut.

Some are the toothachingly sweet desserts that have their origins in the Moorish taste for sweets passed on to the Portuguese. To this Brazilians add an African love of nuts and seeds for crunch and consistency and the abundant sugar and molasses products that the cane-growing northern regions can provide, and voilà, the desserts of Brazil.

Cocada Puxa

Dark Cocada

MAKES 8 SERVINGS

Cocadas are a form of traditional Brazilian dessert that appeals to those who like theirs very sweet. They are usually served in clear glass footed bowls that enable the diner to enjoy not only the taste, but also the variety of colors in the *cocadas*. I first came across *cocadas* at SENAC, a restaurant on the Pelhourinho Square in Bahia. There they graced the luncheon buffet table and I found that, taken in small quantities and counterpointed with fresh fruit rather than the more traditional ambrosia, they can be quite refreshing. Try them served with orange sections.

> **3 cups packed dark brown sugar**
>
> **One 2-inch stick cinnamon**
>
> **3 whole cloves**
>
> **1 cup water**
>
> **3 cups tightly packed freshly grated coconut (see page 37)**

Prepare a thin syrup by mixing the brown sugar, cinnamon, cloves, and water in a large saucepan over medium heat until the sugar dissolves and the mixture is thoroughly combined. Add the coconut and let the mixture cook over low heat, stirring occasionally, until it thickens, about 10 minutes. Pour the *cocada* into a serving bowl, allow to set, and serve it at room temperature.

Cocada Branca

White Cocada

MAKES 8 SERVINGS

Where you see *cocada puxa* in Brazil, *cocada branca* cannot be far behind. This variation on the *cocada* theme allows the diner to savor the difference in taste between the caramely molasses of the brown sugar in the *cocada puxa* and the clove taste of the *cocada branca*.

> 2 cups sugar
>
> 4 whole cloves
>
> 1 cup milk
>
> 2 cups tightly packed freshly grated coconut
> (see page 37)

Bring the sugar, cloves, and milk to a boil in a heavy, medium-size saucepan over medium heat, stirring occasionally. Remove it from the stove and add the grated coconut, mixing it in well. Return the mixture to the stove and cook over low heat, stirring occasionally, until it thickens, about 10 minutes. Pour the *cocada* into a clear glass serving bowl. Chill and serve cold.

Cocada com Abóbora

Pumpkin Cocada

Pumpkin is the unusual ingredient in this *cocada*. While the more traditional Halloween pumpkin can be used, those who live in areas with large West Indian populations will find that the West Indian cooking pumpkin, or calabaza, is actually closer to the pumpkin that Brazilians use. It is a bit firmer in consistency. This orange-hued *cocada* rounds out the trilogy and shows the full range that these coconut confections can take.

> **1 cup peeled and seeded pumpkin pieces,**
>   **about ⅓ pound (see page 28)**
>
> **4 cups water**
>
> **4 whole cloves**
>
> **2 cups sugar**
>
> **2 cups tightly packed freshly grated coconut**
>   **(see page 37)**

In a large, heavy saucepan, cook the pumpkin pieces in the water over medium heat, covered, until they are fork tender, about 15 minutes. Remove the pumpkin pieces and reserve 1 cup of the cooking liquid. Puree the pumpkin in a food processor or food mill and set aside. Place the reserved cooking liquid, cloves, and sugar back in the saucepan and cook over medium heat, stirring occasionally, until the mixture thickens, 7 to 10 minutes. Add the coconut and pumpkin puree, mix well, and cook another 10 minutes. Pour into a glass serving bowl and allow to set. Serve at room temperature.

Ambrosia

———◆———

Brazil's ambrosia is very different from the fruit salad and coconut that many of us know as ambrosia from the southern United States. It is a heavy milk, egg yolk, and sugar mixture that is traditionally served as an accompaniment to *cocadas*.

> **4 cups milk**
>
> **2 cups sugar**
>
> **9 large egg yolks**
>
> **1 tablespoon fresh lemon juice**
>
> **4 whole cloves**

Place the milk in a large saucepan and bring to a boil over medium-high heat; remove it from the heat. Add the sugar, then the egg yolks, one at a time, whisking well to be sure that they are well mixed. Add the lemon juice and cloves and return to the heat. Cook over medium heat for one hour, until the mixture turns golden and becomes grainy. Chill and serve cold with the *cocada*.

Compota de Manga

Mango Compote

MAKES 5 SERVINGS

One of Brazil's favorite ways with tropical fruits is turning them into compotes, or fruits in sugar syrups. Here ripe mangoes provide a taste of the sun. This is a dessert that is best made when the mangoes are at their peak of ripeness.

> **5 large ripe mangoes, peeled and halved with the pit removed (see page 46)**
>
> **2 cups sugar**
>
> **3 whole cloves**
>
> **1½ cups water**

Place all of the ingredients in a large saucepan over low heat and cook for about 20 minutes, stirring occasionally, until you have a thick mixture. Pour into a serving dish, allow to set for about 2 hours, and serve at room temperature.

Compota de Maracujá

Passion Fruit Compote

Compotes can be made with a variety of tropical fruits. If you are fortunate enough to be in an area where you have access to fresh passion fruit, you can serve this compote in which the tartness of the passion fruit harmonizes beautifully with the sweetness of the sugar syrup.

2 pounds passion fruit (see page 46)

1¼ cups water

2 cups sugar

One 1-inch stick cinnamon

3 whole cloves

1 sprig fresh mint

Cut the passion fruit in half and place the pulp in a saucepan with 2 tablespoons of the water. In a large, heavy saucepan, prepare a sugar syrup of the remaining water, the sugar, spices, and mint by boiling them together over medium-high heat, stirring occasionally, for 10 minutes. Add the passion fruit and bring the mixture to a second boil. Pour into a serving dish, cool, and serve.

Doce de Abóbora

Sweet Pumpkin

MAKES 4 SERVINGS

Here, again, pumpkin turns up as a dessert ingredient. This, as with all other Brazilian pumpkin dishes, is made with the pumpkin that is similar to the calabaza, or West Indian cooking pumpkin. If this cannot be found, the old jack-o'-lantern pumpkin can be substituted but will not be as firm; a better bet would be butternut or Hubbard squash.

> **2 pounds pumpkin, peeled, seeded, and cubed (see page 28)**
>
> **2 cups sugar**
>
> **¼ teaspoon ground cloves or to taste**
>
> **½ teaspoon ground cinnamon or to taste**

Wash the pumpkin cubes and place them in a large, heavy saucepan. Cover and cook over low heat until they are fork tender, about 15 minutes. (You do not need to add water.) Remove the pumpkin cubes and puree them in a food processor or food mill. Return the puree to the saucepan with the remaining ingredients and cook over a low heat until you have a stiff, thick paste. Allow the paste to cool and pour into a footed serving bowl. Serve it in dabs with the other sweets and compotes on dessert plates.

Olho de Sogra

Mother-in-law's Eyes

MAKES 4 SERVINGS

Many Brazilian desserts have fanciful names that testify to a wicked Latin sense of humor. My personal candidate for the winner in the names sweepstakes is this stuffed prune dessert called mother-in-law's eyes. The stuffed prunes do have a faint resemblance to the slightly jaundiced stare of a dyspeptic mother-in-law. They're easy to make and guaranteed conversation stoppers.

> 1¼ cups sugar
>
> 1 cup water
>
> 1 cup tightly packed freshly grated coconut (see page 37)
>
> 2 large egg yolks
>
> ½ teaspoon pure vanilla extract
>
> 1 pound pitted prunes
>
> Whole cloves for garnish

Place 1 cup of the sugar, the water, and coconut in a medium-size saucepan and cook over low heat until the mixture thickens, about 15 minutes. Remove the mixture from the stove and let it cool. Whip the egg yolks till lemon-colored and ribboned and add them to the coconut mixture. Add the vanilla, return the mixture to low heat, and cook, stirring, for about 5 minutes. Remove and allow to cool. Spread the prunes open lengthwise. (Slit them lengthwise, if necessary.) Stuff the prunes with the egg-yolk-and-coconut mixture. Dot a clove in the middle of the mixture so that it looks like the pupil of an eye. Roll the prunes in the remaining ¼ cup of sugar and place them in individual paper confectionary cups. Serve these staring confections to your unsuspecting friends.

Quejadinhas

Coconut and Cheese Snacks

MAKES 6 TO 8 SERVINGS

These coconut and Parmesan snacks hover between cocktail treats and desserts. They are what the British would call a savory and are as good at the end of a meal with port or sherry as at the beginning.

1 cup tightly packed freshly grated coconut (see page 37)

One 8-ounce can sweetened condensed milk

2 tablespoons freshly grated Parmesan cheese

2 large egg yolks

Preheat the oven to 450°F. Place all the ingredients in a medium-size bowl and mix well. Drop by the spoonful into small paper pastry cups which have been placed in small muffin tins. Place the muffin tins in a larger roasting pan that has been filled with about 1 inch of water to form a bain-marie and cook for about 35 minutes. The *quejadinhas* will keep well if they are stored in a tightly closed cookie tin.

Baba de Moça

Maiden's Drool

MAKES 4 SERVINGS

Here's another sure winner in the Brazilian dessert-naming competition. The idea behind the name is that this dessert is so good that it makes young girls drool with delight. In some better-bred cookbooks, it's called young girl's delight. This syrupy dessert is a classic one which can be served in cups with a dusting of cinnamon. In Bahia it is eaten with grated Parmesan cheese.

> 1 cup sugar
>
> ½ cup water
>
> 3 large egg yolks
>
> ½ cup thick coconut milk (see page 38)
>
> Ground cinnamon to taste

Prepare a thin syrup by mixing the sugar and water in a small saucepan over low heat. Cook, stirring, for 10 minutes. Remove the syrup from the heat. In a small bowl, drop the egg yolks one by one into the coconut milk while whisking the mixture. Add the egg-yolk-and-coconut-milk mixture to the sugar syrup, return to low heat, and bring to a boil, stirring well until it thickens, about 7 minutes. Serve hot with a dusting of cinnamon.

Arroz Doce

Sweet Rice

MAKES 2 SERVINGS

Sweetened rice desserts seem to be popular in areas where there have been African slaves. One of the Brazilian answers to rice pudding, a traditional dish among many African-American southerners, is this sweetened rice dish.

> 1 cup cooked rice (see page 31)
>
> ¼ cup milk
>
> One 8-ounce can sweetened condensed milk
>
> ¼ cup sugar

Place the cooked rice and milks in a small saucepan and warm over low heat. In a small skillet caramelize the sugar by heating it over low heat while stirring constantly until it is golden brown. Pour the caramel over the rice and mix well. Serve warm.

Canjica de Erminha

Erminha's Canjica

MAKES 4 TO 6 SERVINGS

While discussing Brazilian food one morning with my friend Erminha, conversation turned to the traditional Brazilian dessert *canjica*. The white hominy-and-coconut-milk dish is delicious, but requires the overnight soaking and lengthy cooking of the hominy corn. Why not, we thought, try it with canned hominy as a time-saver. Voilà, *Canjica de Erminha,* a speedy way with a traditional dessert.

> 2 cups thin coconut milk (see page 38)
>
> ½ cup sugar
>
> 4 whole cloves or to taste
>
> One 16-ounce can large white hominy corn
> (Goya is good), drained
>
> Ground cinnamon and toasted grated coconut
> (see note below)

Place the coconut milk, sugar, and cloves in a large, heavy saucepan and bring them to a simmer over low heat. Then add the hominy. Bring the mixture to a second oil and remove from the heat. The *canjica* is served in small bowls with a dusting of ground cinnamon and toasted grated coconut.

NOTE: To toast grated coconut, place it on an ungreased cookie sheet in a thin layer and put under the broiler for 1 to 3 minutes, watching and stirring until it is browned.

Torta de Banana

Banana Pie

MAKES ONE 9-INCH PIE

A market in Rio, in Bahia, or in Belém reveals the range of bananas in Brazil. Most of us who are used to only the ripe yellow ones we see in supermarkets would be astonished by the variety. There are cooking bananas (plantains), tiny sugary sweet finger bananas, red-skinned ones, and, yes, even the yellow ones that we know. Here is one of Brazil's dessert ways with bananas.

4 large ripe bananas, peeled and pureed

½ cup packed light brown sugar

Pinch of salt

1 tablespoon unsalted butter

1 tablespoon fresh lime juice

1 tablespoon ruby port

½ teaspoon ground nutmeg

One 9-inch prebaked pie shell (recipe follows)

¼ cup tightly packed freshly grated coconut (see page 37)

Place the banana puree into a large, heavy saucepan with the sugar, salt, and butter. Stir to mix the ingredients thoroughly and bring to a boil over medium heat. Remove from the heat and let cool. Preheat the broiler. Whip the lime juice, port, and nutmeg into the banana mixture. Pour the mixture into the pie shell and sprinkle the top with the grated coconut. Place the pie under the broiler and cook until the coconut is golden brown, about 2 minutes. Remove and serve warm.

Pie Crust

MAKES ONE 9-INCH CRUST

1 cup all-purpose flour

½ teaspoon salt

⅓ cup chilled lard or 7 tablespoons vegetable
shortening

2 to 3 tablespoons ice water

Place the flour and salt in a bowl and mix them together. Then, using a pastry blender, cut in the lard until the mixture has the consistency of cornmeal. Gradually add the water and continue to mix until the dough comes together. Flatten the dough into a disk, wrap in waxed paper and refrigerate for 30 minutes, until chilled. Preheat the oven to 350°F. Roll the dough out on a lightly floured surface, rotating it and flouring it as needed, to create a 10-inch round. Place the dough in a 9-inch pie plate and crimp the edges of the overhanging portion. Prick the bottom of the pastry shell with a fork. Bake for 30 minutes, until golden brown. Transfer to a rack and allow to cool completely.

Docinhos de Amendoim

Sweet Peanut Cakes

MAKES ABOUT 50 CAKES

West Africans use peanuts in ways other than simply as snack foods. This different approach to the peanut is also found in Brazilian cooking where peanuts turn up in a variety of ways. They are pulverized and used as thickeners in stews like Bahia's *Ximxim de Galinha* (page 184), in salads like *Salada Rita* (page 128), roasted as appetizers, and as candies such as *Paçoca* (recipe follows). Here they are mixed with freshly grated coconut and transformed into petit four–like cakes.

> 1 cup roasted peanuts
>
> 1 cup tightly packed freshly grated coconut (see page 37)
>
> 1 cup granulated sugar
>
> 2 large eggs
>
> ¼ cup confectioners' sugar
>
> ¼ cup shelled whole roasted peanuts for garnish

Place the peanuts in a food processor and pulverize them into a fine powder. (Be careful not to get peanut butter.) Place the peanuts, coconut, granulated sugar, and eggs in a medium-size, heavy saucepan and cook over a low flame for about 30 minutes, stirring from time to time. Pour the peanut mixture out onto a buttered surface and allow it to cool. Cut the mixture into small squares, roll them in the powdered sugar, and decorate the top of each one with a roasted peanut. Place them in individual paper confectionary cups and serve. They will keep for two weeks in a cookie tin.

Paçoca

—— ◆ ——

This peanut-and-sugar confection is a children's treat that can also be enjoyed by adults. It's made by mixing finely ground peanuts with sugar.

1 pound roasted peanuts, shelled and skinned

⅔ cup sugar

½ cup cassava meal (see page 31)

Salt to taste

Place the peanuts in a food processor and grind them until they are a fine powder. (In Brazil, this is traditionally done with a mortar and pestle.) Be careful not to get peanut butter. Gradually add the sugar, cassava meal, and salt. Mix well and place in small pieces of brightly colored cellophane or waxed paper. Store in a tightly covered container.

Pé-de-Moleque

Young Boy's Foot

MAKES ABOUT 40 PIECES

This popular candy is prepared in many ways in Brazil. This is an easy variation which uses a regular cast-iron skillet. A marble sheet for setting the candy is useful, but a thick porcelain platter that has been buttered and placed in the freezer for 5 to 10 minutes to chill can be substituted.

> 1 tablespoon butter
>
> ¼ cup shelled peanuts with skins removed
>
> ¼ cup cashews
>
> 1 cup firmly packed light brown sugar
>
> 1 cup sugar
>
> Pinch of baking soda

Butter the marble slab. Place the nuts on a baking sheet in the oven to warm them. Then place the sugars in the skillet over medium heat and cook, stirring constantly with a wooden spoon until the sugar has melted and become syrupy. (This may take 5 or more minutes. When liquefied, stop.) Add the baking soda, stirring well to make sure that it is mixed thoroughly. Add the sugar syrup to the nuts, stirring to make sure that they are well distributed. Pour the mixture onto the greased surface and allow it to cool. Then lift the brittle off the platter and break it into bite-size pieces.

Stored in a glass jar, this will keep for several weeks, if it lasts that long.

Bejinhos de Coco

Little Coconut Kisses

Here the emperor of Brazilian dessert ingredients, the coconut, meets up with the sweetened condensed milk that is also typical of much Brazilian confectionary.

One 8-ounce can sweetened condensed milk

1 tablespoon unsalted butter

½ cup tightly packed freshly grated coconut (see page 37)

¼ cup confectioners' sugar

Whole cloves for garnish

Place the condensed milk and butter in a small, heavy saucepan and cook them over low heat, stirring occasionally, for about 30 minutes, or until the mixture thickens. Remove the mixture from the heat and allow to cool for about 15 minutes. Stir in the coconut. Pour the mixture onto a well-buttered work surface and form it into balls. Roll the balls in the confectioners' sugar and decorate with the cloves. (If you're struck with the terminal cutes at this stage you can form the *bejinhos* into small happy faces or snowmen.) Store in a tightly covered container.

Beijos de Anjo

Angel Kisses

This classic Brazilian dessert is called angel kisses because the confections are so light. They are made to suit the Brazilian sweet tooth which does not cringe at recipes calling for 36 egg yolks and 2 pounds of sugar.

> **9 large egg yolks**
>
> **2 large egg whites, beaten into stiff peaks**
>
> **2 cups sugar**
>
> **1½ cups water**
>
> **3 drops pure vanilla extract**
>
> **2 whole cloves**

Preheat the oven to 350°F. In a medium-size bowl, beat the egg yolks vigorously until lemon colored. Fold in the egg whites gently. Pour the egg mixture into small muffin tins that have been greased and floured until ⅔ full. Put the muffin tins in the oven and bake for about 15 minutes. Meanwhile, mix the sugar, water, vanilla, and cloves together in a large, heavy saucepan and cook over low heat, stirring occasionally, until it attains a syruplike consistency, about 15 minutes. When the *beijos de anjo* are cooked, unmold them and place them in the sugar syrup. Poach them by cooking them in the sugar syrup over medium-low heat for 15 minutes. Pour the kisses and sugar syrup into a large footed glass bowl. Serve at room temperature, spooning a bit of sugar syrup on each serving.

Pão de Mandioca

Manioc Bread

MAKES 6 TO 8 SERVINGS

Manioc is one of the root tubers that the native Brazilian peoples added to the national diet. The Parmesan cheese came with the Italian immigrants much later. These manioc rolls, therefore, are representative of the mixing that has gone on in the country.

You can make this only if you have access to sweet cassava, or manioc, which can be found in West Indian or Brazilian markets. Be sure to get the *sweet* cassava.

> 5 pounds sweet cassava (see page 30), cut
>   into 2-inch pieces
>
> 2 cups freshly grated Parmesan cheese
>
> 3 tablespoons pure olive oil
>
> 3 large eggs
>
> Salt to taste
>
> 2 cups milk

Five pounds of cassava will produce approximately 3 cups of cassava puree. Place the cassava in a large saucepan with water to cover. Bring to a boil over medium-high heat, then reduce the heat to low and simmer for 30 minutes, until the cassava is fork tender. Remove from the water, allow to cool, peel, and puree in a food mill or a food processor.

Preheat the oven to 350°F. Mix the remaining ingredients, except the milk, together in a large bowl until a dough forms. Knead the dough on a lightly floured surface while adding the milk bit by bit. When the dough is well kneaded and shiny, form it into logs and place them on a well-buttered cookie sheet. Place in the oven and cook for 30 minutes, until golden brown. Serve hot.

Sorvete de Manga

Mango Ice Cream

MAKES 4 SERVINGS

Along the streets of Rio de Janeiro, it is possible to see numerous small boutiques called *sorveteria*. They are ice cream stores specializing in delicious ice creams and sherbets prepared from the bounty of tropical fruit that is available in Brazil. Mangoes are available all year round and are one of the favorite flavors. This is a perfect treat for those who are not fond of the fibrous texture that some mangoes have, as all you get is the pure taste of the mango.

> **9 large ripe mangoes, peeled, pitted, and cut into small pieces (see page 46)**
>
> **½ cup water**
>
> **⅓ cup sugar or to taste**

Reserve the pieces of one mango for garnish, mincing them. Place the remaining mango pieces into a food processor or blender with the water and liquefy them. Add the sugar, blending again to make sure that it is well mixed. Sieve the mixture to remove any pulp and place the strained mango in ice cube trays from which the dividers have been removed. When the mixture begins to freeze (it starts to get slushy), remove it, beat until smooth, and return to the freezer trays. When the mixture has frozen a second time, serve cool in a saucer champagne glass garnished with the reserved minced mango.

Sorvete de Abacate

Avocado Ice Cream

MAKES 4 SERVINGS

While we in northern climes think of avocados as salad food, in Brazil the green globes are more often than not mixed with sugar and served as desserts. Here is an unusual avocado ice cream that is typical of the Brazilian dessert way with avocados.

> 3 medium-size ripe avocados, peeled and
>   pitted
>
> 2 tablespoons milk
>
> ½ teaspoon pure vanilla extract
>
> 1 tablespoon dark rum
>
> 2 large egg whites
>
> ¼ cup sugar
>
> Avocado slices for garnish

Place the avocados in a food processor or blender with the milk, vanilla, and rum and liquefy. In a medium-size bowl, beat the egg whites to stiff peaks, adding the sugar a little at a time. Fold the sugary egg whites into the avocado mixture and place in ice cube trays. When the mixture has begun to freeze, remove and beat it until smooth. Return to the freezer trays and the freezer. When it freezes for a second time, serve cold, garnished with a thin slice of avocado.

Goiaba Batida

Guava Frappe

MAKES 4 SERVINGS

Guavas are a tropical fruit that can be found in many markets preserved in syrup. While you lose the flavor of the fresh guava, you get a bit of the savor of the tropics in this guava dessert.

> **One 16-ounce can guavas in sugar syrup (see page 43)**
>
> **½ teaspoon fresh lemon juice**
>
> **½ cup water**
>
> **2 large egg whites**

Set aside 2 of the guavas and half a cup of the syrup. Place the other guavas and remaining syrup in a medium-size, heavy saucepan with the lemon juice and water and cook over low heat, stirring constantly, for 10 minutes. Pour the mixture into a food processor or blender and process until you have a thick paste. Allow to cool. Whip the egg whites until stiff peaks form, then gently fold them into the guava paste. Place the guava-and-egg mixture into saucer champagne glasses and garnish with a half of the reserved guavas and a drizzle of the syrup. Serve chilled.

Creme de Abacate

Avocado Cream

MAKES 4 SERVINGS

Although served in a stemmed glass, this is thick enough to be a dessert and not a beverage.

> **2 large ripe avocados, peeled and pitted**
>
> **1 tablespoon fresh lime juice**
>
> **⅓ cup firmly packed dark brown sugar**
>
> **1 cup half-and-half**
>
> **2 tablespoons ruby port**
>
> **5 sprigs fresh mint**
>
> **Lemon slices for garnish**

Place the avocados, lime juice, sugar, half-and-half, port, and 1 sprig of the mint in a blender or food processor and blend until well mixed and pureed. Pour into chilled stemmed glasses and garnish with a lemon slice and sprig of fresh mint.

Doce de Banana em Rodinhas

Banana Dessert

MAKES 6 SERVINGS

This simple dessert is an adaptation of one of the recipes that I learned in Bahia from my good friends and teachers, the *Baianas* who cook for Bahiatursa events. The dessert travels well because while many of the exotic fruits of Brazil are unknown even in large metropolitan areas, it's always possible to find bananas. This dessert, then, can give those unfamiliar with Brazil, wherever they are, a taste of Bahia.

> 1 pound firm, ripe bananas, peeled and cut into slices
>
> 2 cups firmly packed light brown sugar
>
> 2 cups water
>
> Ground cinnamon and whole cloves to taste

Place all the ingredients in a large, heavy saucepan and cook over medium-high heat, stirring occasionally, until the syrup has thickened and the bananas turn reddish. Let cool and serve at room temperature in a footed glass bowl.

Abacaxi com Vinho

Pineapple with Red Wine

MAKES 4 TO 6 SERVINGS

Abacaxi is pineapple in Brazil where they have some of the sweetest and most delicious in the world. Brazil also makes some wonderful red wines. When pineapple and red wine come together in this dessert, they show some of the sophistication of the big city side of Brazilian cooking.

1 ripe pineapple

**2 tablespoons firmly packed dark brown
   sugar**

1 cup dry red wine

Cut the green top from the pineapple and reserve it. Core the pineapple, hollow it out, and cut the fruit into small pieces. Reserve the hollowed out pineapple shell and chill it in the refrigerator. In a medium-size bowl, add the brown sugar and red wine to the cut-up pineapple, mix them well, and allow to sit for 1½ hours at room temperature. When ready to serve, spoon the pineapple-and-wine mixture into the hollowed out pineapple, replace the leafy top of the pineapple, and serve.

Quindins

Brazilian Style Coconut Macaroons

MAKES 12 MACAROONS

This Brazilian dessert is my good-luck dessert. I wrote about it for the first time in *Vogue* magazine after having taken my first trip to Brazil. Later, after many other trips to Brazil and many other tastings, I realized just how typical of Brazilian desserts *quindins* are. They are muffin-size macaroons with a jellylike topping of sugar and egg. If the sugar used is white, the top part comes out light yellow in color. With brown sugar, this turns a light brown. I prefer the slightly molassesy taste that brown sugar gives the mixture and forgo the pretty color for the taste. Here, then, are *quindins,* a necessity on any Bahian dessert table.

>   ¾ cup firmly packed light brown sugar
>
>   1 tablespoon unsalted butter, at room
>   temperature
>
>   1 cup tightly packed freshly grated coconut
>   (see page 37)
>
>   5 large egg yolks
>
>   1 large egg white, beaten into stiff peaks

Preheat the oven to 350°F. Mix the sugar, butter, and coconut together in a medium-size bowl. Beat in the egg yolks one at a time, stirring well. Fold in the beaten egg white. Grease 12 large muffin molds and divide the mixture among them. Place the muffin tin in a larger baking pan filled with 1 inch of boiling water to form a bain-marie. Bake them for 35 minutes, or until the *quindins* are firm and golden. Let them cool and remove from the tin. Serve with tea or as dessert.

BEBIDAS

Beverages

THE JOAQUIM NABUCO FOUNDATION is located in the city of Recife and dedicated to the study of the north and the northeast of Brazil. The foundation is the home of a fascinating museum which features everything from colonial furniture to implements used in the sugarcane-growing regions over the centuries. One of my favorite rooms in the museum, and indeed the favorite room of many who visit it, is a room devoted to cachaça. The walls are decorated from bottom to top with an array of bottles and labels which are testimony enough to the variety and popularity of this liquor.

Produced from sugarcane, cachaça is the drink of the people of the northeast. For the slaves and even for the poor today, it provided and still provides an escape from the hardships of daily life. Recently, the more well-to-do have recognized it as a spirit that mixes wonderfully with the bounty of tropical fruits that Brazil has. Cachaça was out of fashion for several years with the elite; it seems, however, that it is coming back. My friend Marcelo keeps decanters of estate-bottled cachaça on his Rio bar. In the restaurant Casa de Gamboa in Bahia they serve a dessert array of liqueurs made from cachaça. None, though, have the variety of bottles as the Museu do Homem do Nordeste. There the bottles tell cachaça's tale. Some have slightly sexy pictures of young women revealing ample amounts of leg and have names like Nega Fulô (Young Slave). Others are named for local animals like Pitú (crayfish) or Jacaré (alligator).

Some of the more refined ones are called *aguardente de cana*, sugarcane brandy. Nega Fulô and Pitú are generally available in specialty liquor shops in the United States, while other brands can be found occasionally. From the drink called *cachimbo*, a cachaça-and-honey beverage traditionally given to mothers who have just given birth, to the *despacho* for Exu, the trickster god of chance (the offering is traditionally placed at crossroads), to the small liqueurs that are served at wakes, cachaça is part of the Brazilian people. Writer Mario Souto Maior, in his essay on cachaça in the guide to the Museu do Homem do Nordeste, writes that cachaça, soccer, and the animal game (*o jogo do bicho* — an illegal lottery) are the principal passions of the Brazilian people.

Caipirinha

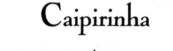

MAKES 1 SERVING

This drink is the leitmotif of many a great Brazilian evening. Prepared with lime sections, sugar, and cachaça, the drink must always be made one at a time. This is wonderful because it allows people to adjust the drink to their liking. Diet-conscious Brazilians even use artificial sugar in their caipirinhas, thinking that it will reduce their caloric intake. When prepared with white rum instead of cachaça, the drink becomes a caipirissima; with vodka, it becomes a caipiroshka.

1 lime, cut into small pieces

Superfine sugar to taste

2 ounces cachaça or white rum to taste

Ice cubes

Place the lime pieces in the bottom of an old-fashioned glass. Add the sugar and crush the lime pieces into the sugar with a pestle. (Crush them pulp-side up, otherwise you get a bitter caipirinha because of too much lime oil.) Add the cachaça and stir to mix. Add the ice cubes, stir again, and serve.

Caipirinha de Maracujá

Passion Fruit Caipirinha

MAKES 1 SERVING

Traditionally a caipirinha is prepared only with limes. However, a current fad in Brazil is preparing caipirinhas with any type of fruit, from oranges to grapes. This one uses the pulp from the passion fruit which adds a refreshing tartness for those like me who do not like their drinks too sweet.

> **1 passion fruit (see page 46)**
>
> **Superfine sugar to taste**
>
> **2 ounces cachaça**
>
> **Ice cubes**

Cut the passion fruit in half and place the pulp and seeds in the bottom of an old-fashioned glass. Add the sugar and crush it into the passion fruit pulp. (Alternately you can strain the seeds out of the liquid and use only the liquid in the drink.) Add the cachaça and ice cubes, stir, and serve.

Batida

MAKES 1 SERVING

In Brazil, this drink is second in popularity only to the caipirinha. The basic difference between a batida and a caipirinha, now that folks are preparing caipirinhas with fruits other than limes, is that batidas use fresh fruit juices while caipirinhas include pulp from or pieces of the fruit. Here the fruit pulp is replaced with freshly grated coconut for a taste that is different from, and to many better than, the cloying coconut taste of the piña colada. Again, batidas are traditionally prepared with cachaça, but they can also be made with white rum.

2 ounces cachaça or white rum

1 tablespoon freshly grated coconut (see page 37)

2 teaspoons superfine sugar or to taste

3 tablespoons crushed ice

Place all the ingredients in a blender or food processor and mix until smooth. Pour into a chilled stemmed cocktail glass. Serve cool. You can garnish the drink with a thin slice of coconut.

Batida Paulista

This is a São Paulo variation on the batida which is smoother and more sophisticated. It's a wonderful way to begin a fancy Brazilian evening.

2 ounces cachaça or white rum

1 tablespoon egg white

Superfine sugar to taste

3 tablespoons fresh lime juice

Place the cachaça, egg white, sugar, and 2 tablespoons of the lime juice into a cocktail shaker with several ice cubes and shake until well mixed. Coat the edge of a stemmed glass with the remaining lime juice and dip it in superfine sugar to coat it. Pour the chilled batida into the glass and serve.

Batida de Morango

Strawberry Batida

MAKES 2 SERVINGS

Because batidas are blended drinks, Brazilians can allow their flights of fruit fancy full range. In this one, fresh ripe strawberries are used along with sweetened condensed milk for a creamy drink.

4 ounces cachaça or white rum

4 or 5 fresh ripe strawberries, washed and hulled

2 tablespoons sweetened condensed milk

2 teaspoons sugar or to taste

Place all the ingredients in a blender or food processor and blend until you have a smooth liquid. Adjust the sugar, if necessary, chill, and serve in chilled stemmed glasses.

Batida de Amendoim

Peanut Batida

MAKES 2 SERVINGS

Roasted peanuts are a favorite Brazilian snack. In this recipe they even get into the drink act. I am not a true fan of peanuts, but for those who enjoy their taste and not their texture, this drink is perfect.

4 ounces cachaça or white rum

3 tablespoons ground roasted peanuts

Superfine sugar to taste

2 tablespoons sweetened condensed milk

Place all the ingredients in a blender or food processor and mix until fully combined. Chill and serve in chilled stemmed cocktail glasses.

Cachimbo

MAKES 1 SERVING

This beverage of honey and cachaça is traditionally given to rural women who have just given birth.

2 ounces cachaça or white rum

3 tablespoons honey

Juice of 1 lime

Mix all the ingredients together in a small, heavy saucepan. Warm them through, over low heat, stirring occasionally. Serve warm in a cup.

Quentão I

Hot Spiced Cachaça I

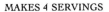

MAKES 4 SERVINGS

This is a warm cachaça drink that is traditionally served during the night of June 24 which honors St. John. In Brazil this festival falls during the cooler winter months. On St. John's Night in many cities and towns of Brazil's northeast, people celebrate the saint's feast day with food, drink, music, and dancing. In Cachoeira, a city in Bahia's backlands, or *Recôncavo*, the festival is particularly noteworthy and townspeople spend days preparing the stalls in which they sell their traditional sweets and other foods. Traditionally, on St. John's Day, young girls can foretell who they are to marry in a variety of ways.

Others can predict future events and even the events of the upcoming year. Bonfires and fireworks are a part of the St. John's Day festivities and one of the beverages that revelers sip as they gather around to watch them is cups of *quentão,* or hot spiced cachaça.

> 1 cup cachaça or white rum
>
> 1 lime, thinly sliced
>
> ½ cup water
>
> 4 whole cloves
>
> One 3-inch stick cinnamon
>
> 1 thumb-size piece fresh ginger, peeled and diced
>
> Superfine sugar to taste

Place all the ingredients in a small nonreactive saucepan and bring them to a boil over medium heat. Strain and serve in mugs or heatproof glasses.

Quentão II

Hot Spiced Cachaça II

MAKES 4 SERVINGS

The name *quentão* comes from the fact that in Portuguese the drink is designed to warm (*esquentar*) those who are celebrating St. John's Night. Here is another variation of this traditional warm beverage which comes from the state of Minas Gerais. Another Minas Gerais version called *crambambali* calls for only cachaça, sugar, lime, and cinnamon.

1 cup boiling water

2 tablespoons honey

1 teaspoon superfine sugar

1 tablespoon minced fresh mint

2 whole cloves

One 2-inch stick cinnamon

1 cup cachaça or white rum

Boil all the ingredients except the cachaça in a small saucepan over medium-high heat for 10 minutes. Strain the mixture, add the cachaça, and return to the saucepan. Heat it thoroughly and serve warm in mugs or heatproof glasses.

Quentão de Vinho

Brazilian Style Mulled Wine

MAKES 12 SERVINGS

This is a drink that takes the place of the traditional *quentão* for those who prefer wine to harder spirits. In this case, it is remarkably like the *vin chaud* of the east of France. Both drinks are perfect après-ski beverages, or good on any cold winter night.

½ cup dry red wine

¼ cup fresh orange juice

2 whole cloves

One 1-inch stick cinnamon

½ lemon, thinly sliced

One 1-inch piece fresh ginger, peeled and
    diced

Superfine sugar to taste

Place all the ingredients in a small nonreactive saucepan and bring to
a boil over low heat. Boil for 5 minutes, then let the *quentão* stand for
30 minutes so the flavors can mix. When ready to serve, reheat the
quentão and serve hot in mugs or heatproof glasses.

Suco de Manga

Mango Juice

MAKES 1 SERVING

Tropical fruit juices are an everyday occurrence in Brazil. In fact, in
Rio the streets are lined with small shops that sell fruit juices of
various kinds. The shops are piled high with mangoes, guavas,
papayas, oranges, limes, pineapples, and other fruits and customers
simply name their preference. In the whirl of a blender, they are
presented with the fresh juice of their choice. This fresh mango juice
will bring the flavor of the tropics to any breakfast table or give you
a different taste from the bottled or canned mango juices you may be
used to.

1 large ripe mango, peeled, pitted, and cut into pieces (see page 46)

½ cup water

Put the mango pieces in a blender or food processor with the water and blend until you have a smooth liquid. Chill and serve.

Suco de Abacaxi e Beterraba

Pineapple-beet Juice

———— ✦ ————

MAKES 1 SERVING

This is one of the more unusual vegetable juices that can be found in the Rio boutiques. The beet juice gives the mixture its deep red color while the pineapple adds its distinctive taste.

1 small beet, peeled and diced

½ cup fresh pineapple chunks

Place the diced beet and pineapple chunks in a blender or food processor and liquefy. Chill and serve. You can garnish this with a pineapple spear if you're serving it as a nonalcoholic cocktail.

Suco de Maracujá

Passion Fruit Juice

MAKES 1 SERVING

I discovered passion fruit on my first trip to Brazil. As a lover of things tart and acid, I was enchanted by its astringent taste. For years, I haunted exotic produce stores and searched the shelves of small bodegas to find passion fruit juice, frozen passion fruit pulp, passion fruit syrups, and other items that bore the flavor that I loved. Now passion fruit have become relatively easy to obtain. They are cultivated in Florida and find their way to exotic fruit markets and specialty stores around the country, and I can enjoy the wonderful tart taste that is so refreshing. The juice is simple to make. I like it tart, so you may wish to dilute it to taste with water.

3 fresh passion fruit (see page 46)

Cold water to taste

Cut the passion fruit open and scoop out the pulp of seeds and gelatinous mass. Place the passion fruit pulp in a strainer and press it through with a pestle or the back of a spoon. Chill the juice. When ready to serve, dilute the juice with water to taste. Serve cold.

Suco de Melancia I

Watermelon Juice I

MAKES 4 SERVINGS

Ripe watermelons are a feature in many northern Brazilian markets. The sweet juicy fruit is eaten in slices as it is here. However, Brazilians, with their craving for fresh fruit juices, also drink watermelon juice, which is remarkably refreshing and simple to prepare.

> **Meat from 1 pound watermelon, seeded and cut into pieces**
>
> **1 cup water**
>
> **4 sprigs fresh mint and 4 watermelon spears for garnish**

Place the watermelon pieces in a blender or food processor with the water and liquefy. Chill and serve cold garnished with a sprig of mint and a watermelon spear.

Suco de Melancia II

Watermelon Juice II

MAKES 4 SERVINGS

This is a second variation on watermelon juice that I discovered when I was trying to research various uses for the fruit. This one is better suited to those who like slightly creamy drinks and frappes.

**Meat from 1 pound watermelon, seeded and
cut into pieces**

¼ cup sweetened condensed milk

4 sprigs fresh mint for garnish

Place the watermelon pieces and condensed milk in a blender or food
processor and process until you have a frothy pink liquid. Chill and
serve over ice, decorated with fresh mint sprigs.

Guaraná

MAKES 1 SERVING

This is a drink that may be difficult to find outside of Brazil and the
occasional Brazilian restaurant, but no Brazilian cookbook would be
complete without a mention of it. Guaraná is a tropical plant that is
used for medicinal purposes and can be found in powdered form in
health food stores. It is also the basis for a soft drink that has a taste
that slightly resembles cream soda, but packs a wallop of caffeine. In
this caffeine-loving nation (see *Cafezinho,* page 257), guaraná is a
very popular soft drink. However, those who are caffeine sensitive
may wish to abstain. Guaraná in cans is occasionally available at
Brazilian shops.

1 can guaraná

Chill the can, then pop the top, pour, and sip. It's that simple.
However, if you're sensitive to caffeine, as I am, you may spend a
sleepless night in payment for this indulgence.

Maté

Brazilian Tea

MAKES 1 SERVING

This beverage is connected with the gauchos of Argentina in the minds of many people. However, the plant from which the tea is made is also a native of parts of Brazil. The tea is indeed consumed by the Brazilian gauchos who, like their Argentinian counterparts, drink it as a fortifier. In Brazil the tea is a part of the folklore of the gauchos of the provinces of Rio Grande do Sul, Santa Catarina, Paraná, and Mato Grosso. *Maté* is available in many health food stores. And while you will probably not be sipping it through a silver straw called a *bomba* from the traditional gourd, or *chimarrão*, on the pampas, you'll still be able to savor the taste of the Brazilian gauchos. Remember, though, it does contain caffeine.

Maté comes in various strengths, so the best bet is to follow the package instructions for brewing. Serve hot, in the traditional manner, or chilled with ice cubes.

Cafezinho

Brazilian Coffee

Coffee is the oil that makes the wheels of commerce move in Brazil. It is impossible to sit in any office or shop for more than five minutes without someone asking you if you want a tiny cup of coffee, *"Você quer um cafezinho?"* The day goes by with that cry as the leitmotif and caffeine-sensitive Americans like myself can spend the entire day debating whether to take the coffee and lose the sleep or to offend by refusing. At times, it is quite a dilemma. I solve the problem by reminding myself that Brazilian coffee is delicious and it comes in a very small cup each time. Somehow that seems to work, for I rarely have caffeine-related loss of sleep problems in Brazil.

Coffee brewing is a matter of personal preference, but many Brazilians still use a fabric coffee filter. However, whatever your preferred method, remember, it must be 100 percent Brazilian coffee.

Some other Brazilian brewing techniques to remember are:
• Once prepared, coffee must not be reheated and should be served within an hour.
• Purchase coffee in small quantities and try to buy it fresh weekly.
• Coffee should always be served boiling hot.
• Don't stint on the coffee. One heaping tablespoon per cup of water is a good Brazilian guideline.
• Brazilians like their coffee sweet, though many of the city folk are now turning to artificial sweeteners. Adjust the sugar, if any, to your own taste.

Agua de Coco

Coconut Water

MAKES 1 SERVING

Coconut water is one of the most refreshing beverages available anywhere in the tropics and Brazil is no exception. Along the beaches of Rio, Bahia, and other points in the northeast are stands selling chilled green coconuts. The vendor lops off the top of the coconut with a machete, inserts a straw, and *voilà*, tropical bliss. Coconut water is also excellent when mixed with cachaça or white rum and has a reputation for being the perfect hangover cure. (I'm not telling.) We, in northern climes, are not lucky enough to have a stand on every street corner selling this nectar. However, those who, like myself, live near or in neighborhoods with large West Indian populations will revel in the fact that with each passing summer, coconut water seems to become more available. I get mine in gallon jugs from my neighborhood vendors with their sharp machetes and bunches of chilled green coconuts. You may find canned coconut water in specialty supermarkets. This, however, is not the same thing as it is usually imported from the Far East and has been presweetened, thereby losing its true fresh taste.

Caipim Limão

Citronella

———— ◆ ————

Citronella, or lemon grass, is an herbal tea that is frequently consumed after meals because it aids in digestion. This tea, which does indeed have the familiar fragrance of the mosquito-repellent candles that you remember from childhood barbecues, is delicious and a very soothing after-dinner beverage. Citronella is packaged in a variety of ways, from tea bags to dried grass stalks. Most are available at health food stores and should be prepared according to package directions. The lemony scented tea should be left to infuse for several minutes. You'll know when it's ready because it will scent the area with its fragrance.

Licor de Mel

Honey Liqueur

MAKES 6 TO 8 SERVINGS

There is a whole Brazilian school of preparing liqueurs and after-dinner cordials. The preparation of these liqueurs takes months and is done meticulously by those who are proud of their kitchen skills. When ready, they are lovingly preserved and presented after dinner in cut crystal and blown glass decanters. Liqueurs are prepared from tropical fruits, from coffee and tea, and from spices and herbs. This one is prepared from honey.

> 3 cups vodka
>
> 4 teaspoons minced orange zest
>
> 3 whole cloves
>
> Pinch of ground cinnamon
>
> 2 cups honey
>
> 3 cups water

Place the vodka and zest in a large, loosely stoppered glass jar and allow to soak for a month in a cool, dark place. Then add the cloves, cinnamon, honey, and water, pour into a large nonreactive saucepan, and cook over low heat for 10 minutes. Remove the mixture from the heat and allow it to cool. Pour it back into the loosely stoppered glass jar. Allow the liqueur to rest for a week in a cool, dark place, shaking it occasionally to make sure all of the ingredients are well mixed. Finally, filter the liqueur through cheesecloth and pour it into a tightly stoppered bottle. Allow it to rest for another month and then serve, after dinner, in cordial glasses.

Mata Nego

Man Killer

MAKES 1 QUART

This drink's name gives some idea of its potency. The mixture in itself is enough to make the strong pale. It's simple to make and spring on your unsuspecting friends. Go sparingly, though, you may need them the next day.

> 1 quart cachaça or white rum
>
> 2 tablespoons finely ground Brazilian coffee
>
> 1 tablespoon crushed aniseed
>
> 6 whole cloves
>
> 1 tablespoon crushed black tea
>
> ½ cup cognac
>
> 2 ounces Fernet Branca or other bitters

Mix all the ingredients together in a loosely stopped glass bottle and store for two to three months in a cool, dark place. Strain into a decanter. Serve to the stalwart with a warning.

UM GOSTO DO BRASIL

A Taste of Brazil

WHEN PAGING through a cookbook, it is easy to know which recipes you'll cook right away and which ones may never make it to your table. Sometimes, though, it is a bit more difficult to decide how to combine dishes and how to put together a complete dinner. Here are some menu suggestions to give you a taste of Brazil. Also included are suggestions for decorations and even possible musical selections.

SATURDAY ON THE BEACH IN RIO

Caipirinha (page 244)

Feijoada (page 171)

Fresh tropical fruit

If you're doing this as a summer party, you might ask guests to all come in their bathing suits, and decorate with beach umbrellas and paper kites. In the winter, you might want to enjoy a video of *Blame It on Rio* or *Flying Down to Rio* and present guests with a travel folder on Brazil (available at no charge from your travel agent) so that they can dream. For music, try to find one of the records from the samba school parades from any year's carnival or a vintage Carmen Miranda album.

BAHIAN BASH

Caipirinha de Maracujá (page 245)

Casquinha de Siri (page 83)

Ximxim de Galinha (page 184)

Quindins (page 240)

Lacy tablecloths set with wooden plates and earthenware bowls will set the scene. For table decorations, think of a horn of plenty of tropical fruits. For music, try for recordings by Maria Bethania, Gal Costa, Caetano Veloso, or Gilberto Gil.

FESTA DE SÃO JOÃO

Tutú a Mineira made up of

the beans—Tutú a Mineira (page 144)

the kale—Couve a Mineira (page 142)

the pork chops—Costeletas de Porco (page 181)

Quentão (page 249)

June 24 is Saint John's Night in much of the northeast. It is a night of magic, with fireworks, fortune-telling and the hot cachaça or wine drink called *quentão*. Approximate it at home using sparklers to decorate the table and by having someone read the tea leaves for your guests. For music, who else but the most famous Minero—Milton Nacimento.

SÃO PAULO SOPHISTICATION

Batida Paulista (page 247)

Cuscuz Brasileiro (page 81)

Camarões a Paulista (page 203)

Abacaxi com Vinho (page 239)

The bright lights of Brazil's most prosperous city come to life when you bring out the fine china and the silver candlesticks. Add a lace tablecloth and Villa-Lobos on the CD player and voilà.

HOMENAGEM AOS GAUCHOS

Mata Nego (page 261)

Churrasco (page 176)

Fresh Fruit

Maté (page 257)

This is a good way to theme a summer barbecue. Remember, though, to offer alternative beverages for those who are caffeine sensitive — the *mata nego* and the *maté* are both full of it. As alternatives, try a simple glass of good cachaça or aguardente de cana instead of the *mata nego* and a Caipim Limão, or citronella (see page 259), after dinner.

A GAROTA DE IPANEMA LUNCHEON

Suco de Melancia (page 255)

Sardinhas Grelhadas (page 193)

Salada Mixta (page 132)

I contend that the girl from Ipanema must be on a constant diet, so this light luncheon in her honor can be decorated with calorie-counting charts and tape measures.

FORTALEZA FISH FRY

Suco de Manga (page 252)

Peixe Frita Fortaleza (page 192)

Salada de Palmito (page 123)

Sorvete de Abacate (page 235)

Fortaleza is known for its fine linens, but this is not a good time to break out your best tablecloth. Opt for a simple cloth one. Basic, colorful place settings will re-create the feel of the open air seaside restaurants along the beach. For music, any simple, soothing music will do.

A BAHIAN DESSERT TABLE

Quindins (page 240)

Ambrosia (page 217)

Doce de Abóbora (page 220)

Cocada Branca (page 215)

Cocada Puxa (page 214)

Bring out the lace cloth again. This time, you'll arrange footed glass bowls of the multihued sweets on it, along with dessert plates and silver spoons. You may find that you'll want to add fresh fruit drinks and homemade liqueurs to the table for a full spread.

FOOD FOR THE GODS — AN
AFRO-BAHIAN DINNER

Cachaça (page 33)

Acarajé (page 59)

Ximxim de Galinha (page 184)

Canjica de Erminha (page 224)

This meal is comprised of foods that are also served in ritual form in the *terreiros* of Bahia. The *orixás* that they are for are, respectively, Exu, the trickster; Yansã, the goddess of tempests; Oxum, the goddess of love and money; and Oxalá, the wise god of creativity.

Mail-order Sources

Many Brazilian items can be found in supermarkets in urban areas. Specialty items such as palm oil and cassava meal can be located in shops selling Latin American items. In New York City, Little Brazil, the block of 46th Street between 5th and 6th avenues, offers several Brazilian shops and restaurants. Some of the shops do a mail-order business.

COISA NOSSA
46 West 46th Street
New York, NY 10036
(212) 719-4779
Brazilian specialty items such as *dendê* (palm oil) and malagueta peppers. Also Brazilian records and tapes.
Free mail-order catalog

PALISADES WHOLESALERS
6500 Dewey Avenue
West New York, New Jersey
(201) 854-3964
Latin American food items.

SHEPHERD'S GARDEN SEEDS
Shipping Office
30 Irene Street
Torrington, CT 06790
(203) 482-3638
Seeds and information on growing your
own chiles and other special
vegetables and herbs

Index